From Your Friends At **The MAILBOX**®

NOVEMBER

A MONTH OF REPRODUCIBLES AT YOUR FINGERTIPS!

Grades 2–3

D1611621

Project Editor:
Amy Erickson

Editor:
Darcy Brown

Writers:
Darcy Brown, Rebecca Brudwick, Amy Erickson,
Kimberly Fields, Cynthia Holcomb, Nicole Iacovazzi,
Njeri Jones, Mary Lester

Art Coordinator:
Clevell Harris

Artists:
Cathy Spangler Bruce, Pam Crane,
Teresa Davidson, Nick Greenwood,
Clevell Harris, Sheila Krill, Rob Mayworth,
Kimberly Richard, Barry Slate,
Donna K. Teal

Cover Artist:
Jennifer L. Tipton

www.themailbox.com

©1999 by THE EDUCATION CENTER, INC.
All rights reserved.
ISBN10 #1-56234-292-4 • ISBN13 #978-156234-292-0

Manufactured in the United States
10 9 8 7 6 5 4

Table Of Contents

November Free Time

Monday	Tuesday	Wednesday	Thursday	Friday
List your classmates who have November birthdays. Write a birthday message for each student on his special day. 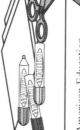	Election Day is the first Tuesday after the first Monday in November. Ask each of ten friends to vote for her favorite lunch on this week's school menu. Count the votes; then write three sentences about the results. 	Yum! November 3 is Sandwich Day! For each letter of the alphabet, write a different type of sandwich. Draw a heart beside the name of your favorite sandwich. 	It's Peanut Butter Lovers' Month! How are a peanut and a book alike? Write your answer on another sheet of paper. 	November is Child Safety And Protection Month. Make a poster of at least three classroom safety rules.
Cat Week is the first full week of November. Imagine that you are a cat on a cold, rainy night. Write a story about your evening. Meow! 	The windshield wiper was patented on November 10, 1903, by Mary Anderson. If you could invent something for cars, what would it be? Write and illustrate your idea.	Celebrate author William Steig's November 14 birthday by reading one of his books, such as *Doctor DeSoto* (Farrar, Straus & Giroux, Inc.; 1990) or *Sylvester And The Magic Pebble* (Aladdin Paperbacks, 1987).	National Children's Book Week is the third week of November. Design a snazzy new cover for your favorite book. 	American Education Week is the week before Thanksgiving. Write a paragraph that explains why going to school is important. 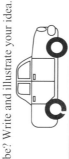
On November 21, 1783, people flew in a hot-air balloon for the first time. Benjamin Franklin saw the event. Write an entry for his diary telling about it.	In 1990, Clifford® The Big Red Dog® was in the Macy's Thanksgiving Day Parade® for the first time. Draw a picture of another book character you would like to see in the parade.	There are ten pies for Thanksgiving. Some are apple and some are pumpkin. How many of each kind could there be? Show as many different answers as you can. 	Kevin Henkes was born on November 27. He has written and illustrated books about many characters, such as Lilly and Chester. Draw a picture of a new character for his books. Write a paragraph describing him or her. 	How many words can you write using just the letters in the words *Happy Thanksgiving*? Write as many as you can.
Pretend that you and a friend are camping in the woods for a week. If you could only take ten things, what would you take? List them on a sheet of paper. 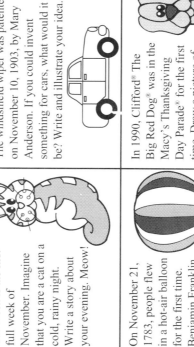	Write at least ten words that have *th* like in *thank* or *toothbrush*. Draw a star beside each word that has exactly two syllables. **TH**	November is the 11th month of the year. Write at least five number sentences for 11. **+ ? =**	Turkey again? Write a paragraph about your favorite way to eat leftover turkey.	Look at a calendar to find out how many days are left in the year. If you had a penny for each day, how much more money would you need to make a dollar? 

Note To The Teacher: Have each student staple a copy of this page inside a file folder. Direct students to store their completed work in their folders.

November
Events And Activities For The Family

Directions: Select at least one activity below to complete as a family by the end of November.
(Challenge: See if your family can complete all three activities.)

Peanut Butter Lovers' Month

Celebrate Peanut Butter Lovers' Month by comparing homemade and store-bought peanut butter! With your youngster's help, make a batch of homemade peanut butter (see the recipe shown). Then have your child spread the peanut butter on crackers and place the treats on a plate. Ask your youngster to prepare crackers with store-bought peanut butter in a like manner and place them on a different plate. Have each family member sample both types of peanut-butter crackers and vote for the one he or she likes best. Then help your child make a bar graph of the results and post it on the refrigerator. Mmmm! November *is* a mouthwatering month!

Homemade Peanut Butter
(Makes 1 cup)

Ingredients:
2 cups shelled peanuts
2 tablespoons vegetable oil

Directions:
Place the ingredients in a food processor or blender. Blend the mixture until it is smooth. Spoon the peanut butter into a small bowl or dish.

Bag It!

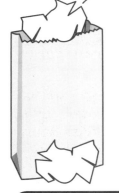

James Naismith, the inventor of the game of basketball, was born on January 6, 1861. To honor his birthday, play an indoor version of this sport with your family. Place a large paper bag on a table and place a small, heavy item in the bag to keep it from moving during the game. Wad several sheets of scrap paper. Determine if you will play the game as individuals or as teams. Then have each player, in turn, stand a designated distance from the bag and try to throw a wad of paper into it. For each "basket" made, a team or individual earns a letter in the name *Naismith.* The first team or individual who spells *Naismith* wins. For added fun, try more difficult shots, such as shooting the paper wads backwards, left-handed, or with eyes closed. What a lively way to work on eye-hand coordination!

Thanksgiving Placemats

Here's a fun craft idea for decorating your Thanksgiving table in fine style! At least one day before Thanksgiving, have each household member weave one or more placemats by following the directions provided. Happy Thanksgiving!

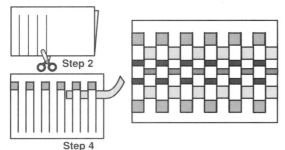

Step 2

Step 4

Woven Placemat
Materials For One Placemat:
two 12" x 18" sheets of colored construction paper (if desired, use two different colors)
scissors
ruler
glue
yarn and curling ribbon (optional)
Directions:
1. Fold one sheet of construction paper in half lengthwise.
2. From the fold, cut one-inch slits, being careful to leave a one-inch border around the edges (see the illustration).
3. From the second sheet of construction paper, cut lengthwise strips of varying widths.
4. Weave the strips of construction paper through the slits on the first sheet as shown. If desired, weave lengths of ribbon and yarn, too. Trim lengths to the size of the mat.
5. Glue the ends of the strips, yarn, and ribbon to the mat. Allow the glue to dry.

Note To The Teacher: Give one copy of this reproducible to each student at the beginning of the month. Encourage each family to complete at least one activity by the end of November.

BRAVO FOR BOOKS!

Explore the wonderful world of books with these "paws-itively" delightful activities! "Tail-or" made for celebrating National Children's Book Week (the third week in November), these ideas will have your students begging for more!

Bone Up On Books!

Here's a "bone-afide" reading motivation idea! Give each student a copy of the dog bowl pattern on page 6. Have him personalize and color the bowl as desired. Then instruct him to carefully cut along the dotted line. Staple students' prepared dog bowls onto a bulletin board titled "Bone Up On Books!" Duplicate a desired number of the bone patterns (page 6) on white construction paper. Cut out the patterns and place them in an envelope near the display. Each time a student finishes reading a book, have him write the title on a bone cutout and slide the cutout into the slit on his dish. After he has read a specified number of books, present each youngster with a prepared copy of the award on page 6. No doubt students will love seeing their "bone-anza" of reading accomplishments grow and grow!

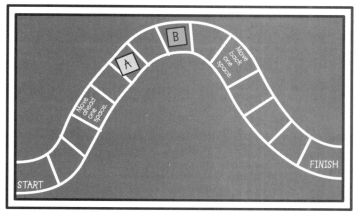

Top Dog Trivia

With this fast-paced trivia game, tongues will be a-waggin' with talk of great books! To prepare, draw and label on the chalkboard a gameboard similar to the one shown. Have each student write on an index card three clues about her favorite book. Instruct her to write the book title on the back of the card. Collect, shuffle, and place the cards faceup in a stack. Divide students into two or more teams and assign each team a letter. For each team, label a different-colored construction-paper square with its letter, and tape the resulting game piece onto the Start space.

To play, draw a card for the first player on a team and read the clues aloud. If the player correctly identifies the book described, with the help of her team members, advance her team's game piece one space. Then place the card in a discard pile. If she gives an incorrect answer, return the card to the bottom of the stack. Move the game piece as directed if it lands on a space with a direction. Play continues with the remaining players in a like manner until one team reaches Finish. (If necessary, provide clues for additional titles until a winner is declared.) Celebrate a job well done by reading aloud to students a favorite book.

Read And Roll

Student learning will be on a roll with this story-cube idea! Cover an empty square-shaped box with brightly colored gift wrap. Label one side with each of the following words: "author," "illustrator," "main characters," "setting," "plot," and "favorite part." Ask students to sit in a circle on the floor. Have each student, in turn, roll the prepared story cube. Name one of the books the class has read; then ask the student to identify the story information that corresponds with the side rolled. Vary this activity by making different story cubes with labels such as "problem," "solution," and "what might happen in a sequel."

Patterns And Student Award
Use with "Bone Up On Books!" on page 5.

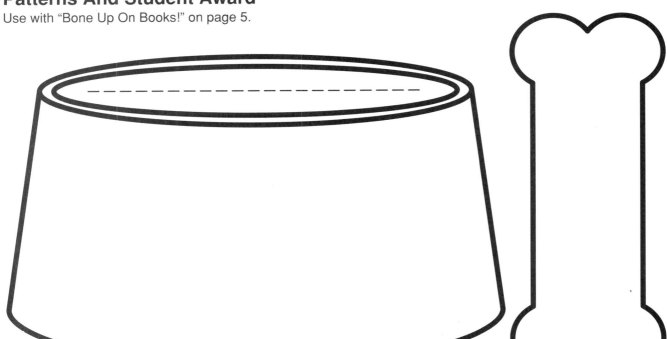

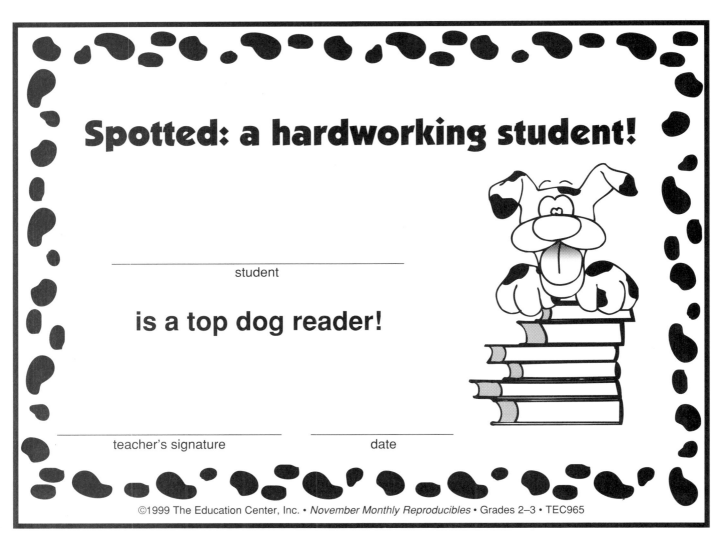

Spotted: a hardworking student!

_____
student

is a top dog reader!

_____   _____
teacher's signature   date

Dog Reading Log

Write your name on the collar.
Color the dog, leaving the spots blank.
Cut out the dog and glue it onto a
    sheet of paper.
Each time you read a book,
    write the title and date
    on a spot.

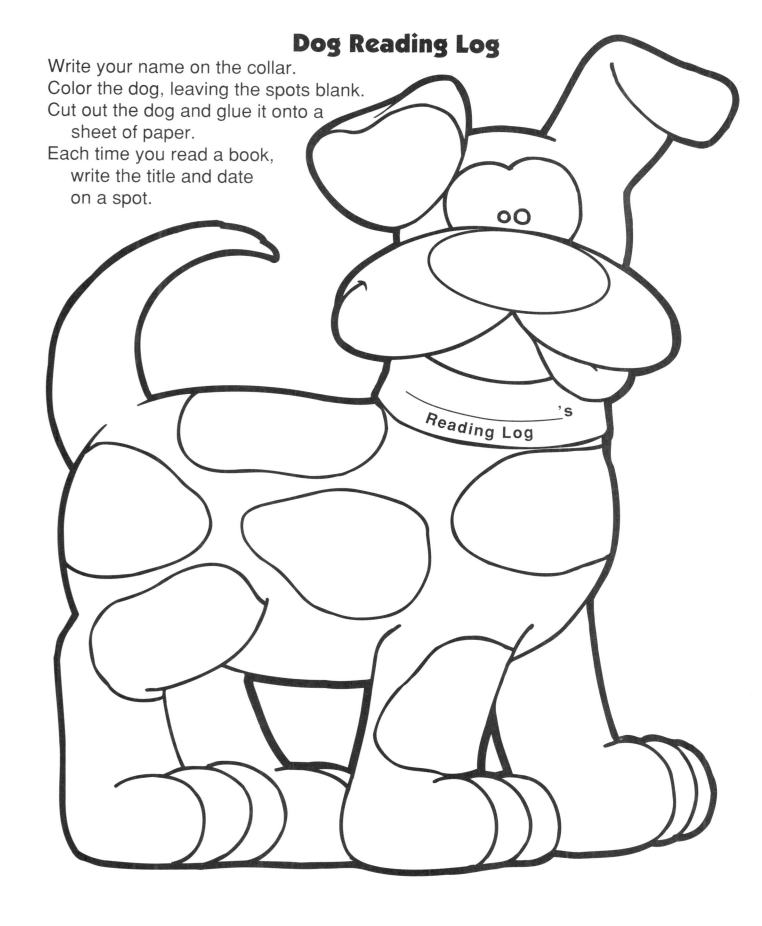

Reading Log 's

Note To The Teacher: Each student will need a sheet of colored construction paper, crayons, glue, and scissors to complete this activity.
If desired, display each student's completed reading log or store it in a portfolio to track his progress.

Bookmark Patterns

Reading is "paws-itively" fun!

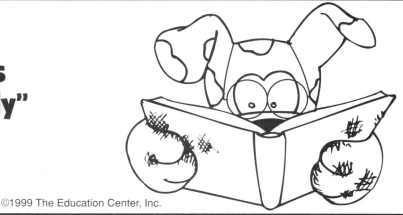

©1999 The Education Center, Inc.

Make no bones about it! I love to read!

_____
Name

©1999 The Education Center, Inc.

Track down a good book today!

©1999 The Education Center, Inc.

Read any good "tails" lately?

Try these popular pooch stories.

Duke The Dairy Delight Dog
by Lisa Campbell Ernst
(Simon & Schuster Books
For Young Readers, 1996)

Walter's Tail
by Lisa Campbell Ernst
(Aladdin Paperbacks, 1997)

Rugby & Rosie
by Nan Parson Rossiter
(Dutton Children's Books, 1997)

Henry And Mudge Get The Cold Shivers
by Cynthia Rylant
(Simon & Schuster Trade, 1996)

©1999 The Education Center, Inc.

©1999 The Education Center, Inc. • *November Monthly Reproducibles* • Grades 2–3 • TEC965

8   **Note To The Teacher:** Duplicate the bookmarks and distribute them to students as desired.

ELECTION DAY

The results are in! This Election Day unit is a surefire winner!

On The Campaign Trail

It will be a race to the White House with this partner campaign-trail game! Invite students to share what they already know about the presidential election process. Then refer to page 11 to provide students with additional information. Next give each student one copy each of pages 10 and 11. Have him cut apart his game cards and answer key and store them in a small resealable plastic bag. Pair students and give each youngster a small game piece such as a plastic counter or a coin. To play, each twosome uses one set of cards and an answer key, and each student uses his own gameboard. One student shuffles the cards and places them facedown. In turn, each youngster draws a card, reads aloud the sentence, and identifies the missing word. His partner uses the answer key to verify his response. If it is correct, the card is placed in a discard pile, and the player rolls a die. He moves his game piece ahead one space if he rolls an odd number and two spaces if he rolls an even number. If he is incorrect, the card is placed at the bottom of the stack, and the player does not move his game piece. If a player lands on a space with one or more stars, he follows the directions. The first player to reach Finish, the White House, wins (have students reshuffle and restack the cards as necessary). For extra reinforcement of election information, encourage each youngster to play his game with family members too. The race is on!

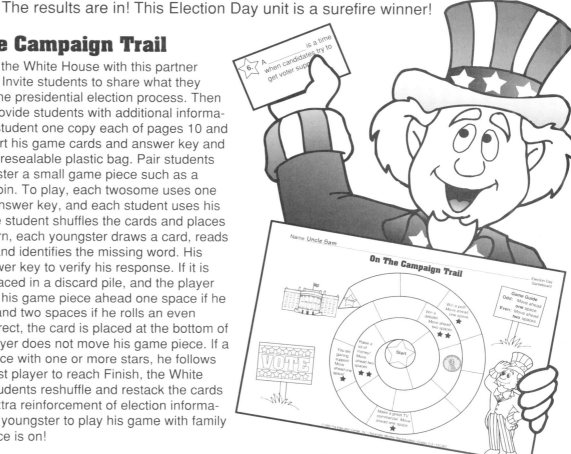

And The Winner Is...

What better way to help students understand the election process than by having a classroom election? With students' help, select a controversial topic they care about, such as whether there should be one long recess or two short ones or what book the class will read next. Help students divide into "parties" in support of their viewpoints. For each party, have a student assume the role of candidate to represent the issue and assign one or more youngsters to each of the following roles: campaign manager (organizes the campaign), media consultant (makes advertising decisions), research aide (researches facts about the issue), speech writer (helps the candidate prepare his speeches), and volunteer worker (completes any other tasks needed to promote the candidate). Set aside time each day until a predetermined election date for each party to campaign. Then on class election day, instruct students to vote by secret ballot. Count the votes with students' help to determine a winner. Give the candidate from each party an opportunity to make a congratulatory or victory speech. Then celebrate everyone's hard work with a snack of juice and red, white, and blue decorated cupcakes.

Name

On The Campaign Trail

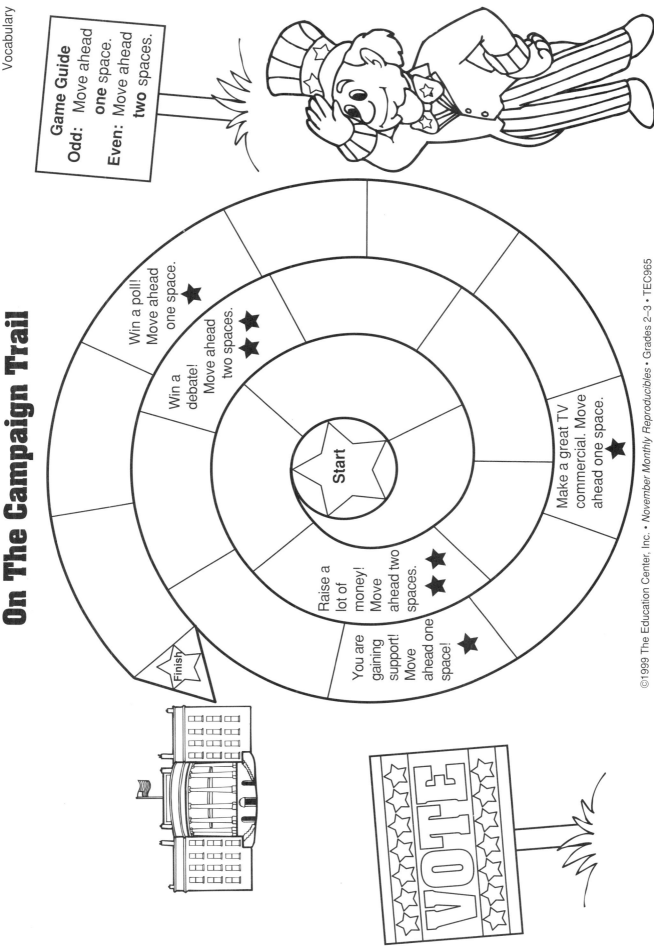

Game Guide
Odd: Move ahead **one** space.
Even: Move ahead **two** spaces.

Start

Win a poll! Move ahead one space.

Win a debate! Move ahead two spaces.

Make a great TV commercial. Move ahead one space.

Raise a lot of money! Move ahead two spaces.

You are gaining support! Move ahead one space!

Finish

VOTE

Note To The Teacher: Use with "On The Campaign Trail" on page 9.

10

★ 1. A person must be at least _____ years old to vote.	★ 2. The president of the United States is elected every _____ years.	★ 3. Most U.S. elections are held in the month of _____.
★ 4. A list of candidates is called a _____.	★ 5. If a person is away on Election Day, he can vote by _____ ballot.	★ 6. A _____ is a time when candidates try to get voter support.
★ 7. The mascot of the Democratic party is a _____.	★ 8. The mascot of the Republican party is an _____.	★ 9. A _____ is a study that finds out how people feel about something.
★ 10. An _____ is a voting process.	★ 11. To be a U.S. president, a person must be at least _____ years old.	★ 12. Many places in the United States use voting _____ instead of paper ballots.
★ 13. A person must be a _____ of the United States to vote in this country.	★ 14. The president's wife is called the _____.	★ 15. A person who is trying to get elected is called a _____.
★ 16. Most people go into a voting _____ to vote.	★ 17. A political _____ is a group of people who have similar ideas about government.	★ 18. After being elected, the new president starts his job in the month of _____.

Answer Key

1. 18
2. four
3. November
4. ballot
5. absentee
6. campaign
7. donkey
8. elephant
9. poll
10. election
11. 35
12. machines
13. citizen
14. first lady
15. candidate
16. booth
17. party
18. January

©1999 The Education Center, Inc. • *November Monthly Reproducibles* • Grades 2–3 • TEC965

Note To The Teacher: Use with "On The Campaign Trail" on page 9.

Name _____

Campaign Shopping

Study the items in the Campaign Store.
Read each problem.
Solve the problem in its box.
Write the answer in the blank star beside it.
Use the Color Code to outline each problem's stars.

Campaign Store

$.55	$.69	$.75	$.85	$.95	$1.10	$1.50	$1.75
button	bumper sticker	key chain	poster	hat	flag	box of pencils	bunch of balloons

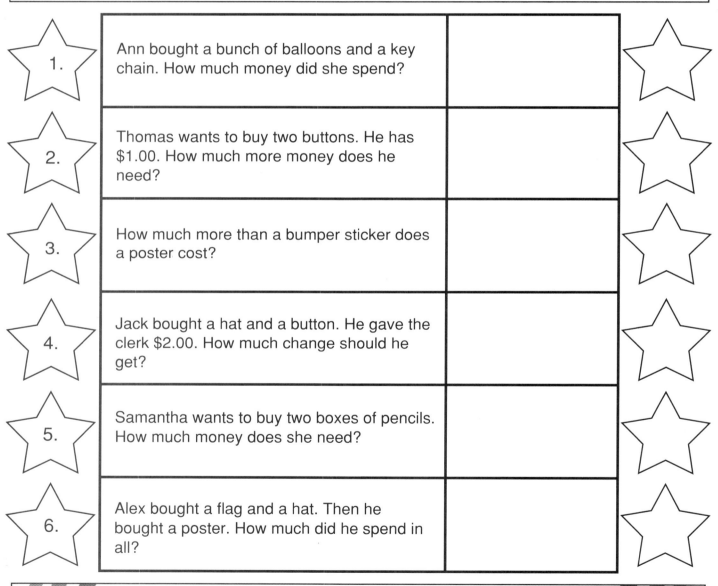

1. Ann bought a bunch of balloons and a key chain. How much money did she spend?

2. Thomas wants to buy two buttons. He has $1.00. How much more money does he need?

3. How much more than a bumper sticker does a poster cost?

4. Jack bought a hat and a button. He gave the clerk $2.00. How much change should he get?

5. Samantha wants to buy two boxes of pencils. How much money does she need?

6. Alex bought a flag and a hat. Then he bought a poster. How much did he spend in all?

Color Code

If the answer is **less** than $.75, outline the problem's stars with **blue.**
If the answer is **more** than $.75, outline the problem's stars with **red.**

MARC BROWN

It's birthday month for author-illustrator Marc Brown, whose special day is November 25! Brown has endeared himself to readers through his tales of a young aardvark named Arthur, his friends, and his family. Because these characters evolved as Brown told stories to his children, it's no surprise that youngsters everywhere readily identify with them. Use these awesome aardvark activities for a class celebration of this author and his popular children's books!

Arthur Then And Now

Many things change with time, and the beloved Arthur character is no exception. Use this critical-thinking activity to explore with students how this adorable aardvark has been modified. In advance, gather several books in the Arthur series and place them in a prominent classroom location (see "Marvelous Marc Brown Books" on this page for suggestions). Divide a sheet of chart paper into three columns, and label the columns "1," "2," and "3." Write each of the following titles at the top of a different column: *Arthur's Nose* (Little, Brown And Company; 1976), *Arthur's Eyes* (Little, Brown And Company; 1979), and *Arthur's Chicken Pox* (Little, Brown And Company; 1994). Then ask students to pay particular attention to the illustrations as you read aloud each of these books. Next have students describe how Arthur looks in each book as you record their responses below the corresponding title on the prepared chart. Invite students to share their ideas about the reasons Marc Brown has modified the character. Then each time students read an Arthur book, have them identify which of the three listed books the illustrations are most like. To extend this activity, have each student choose two of the listed books, then compare and contrast them with a Venn diagram.

Fabulous Favorites

Whether it's Arthur's troubles on his rainy family vacation or as he trains his puppy, students are sure to have a favorite Arthur episode. Feature students' most-loved Arthur books with this story grammar idea. Give each youngster a copy of page 14 and six 3 1/2" x 4" pieces of drawing paper. Have him add features to the character to resemble Arthur. Then ask him to personalize and color his booklet pattern as desired, leaving the center box blank. Instruct each student to cut out his page headings and glue each one near the top of a separate piece of drawing paper. Ask the student to write information about his favorite Arthur book on each piece of paper to correspond with its heading. Instruct him to add illustrations; then have him complete the sentence on his booklet pattern. Have each youngster stack his pages in the following order: title, main characters, setting, problem, solution, and favorite part. Then ask him to staple the pages to his booklet pattern where indicated. Give each student an opportunity to share his work; then, if desired, help youngsters create a class graph of their favorite titles.

Marvelous Marc Brown Books

Arthur's Family Vacation (Little, Brown And Company; 1998)
Arthur Goes To Camp (Little, Brown And Company; 1998)
Arthur's New Puppy (Little, Brown And Company; 1995)
Arthur's TV Trouble (Little, Brown And Company; 1997)
Arthur Writes A Story (Little, Brown And Company; 1996)
D.W. Thinks Big (Little, Brown And Company; 1995)

Favorite Book Patterns

Use with "Fabulous Favorites" on page 13.

Page Headings

Title
Main Characters
Setting

Page Headings

Problem
Solution
My Favorite Part

Booklet Pattern

_____ 's

Favorite Arthur Book

I like this book because

_____

_____

_____

_____

_____

_____

©1999 The Education Center, Inc.

What A Character!

In each frame, draw and color a different
   character from an Arthur book.
Write the character's name below the frame.

List four things that tell about each character.

1. _____   1. _____
2. _____   2. _____
3. _____   3. _____
4. _____   4. _____

Think about your lists.
Then complete the sentence below.

I am more like _____ than _____

because _____

_____.

Bonus Box: Choose one of the characters from above. On the back of this sheet, write a new story
about the character.

Note To The Teacher: Share with students several Arthur books before assigning this activity. See "Marvelous Marc Brown Books" on
page 13 for suggested titles.

Name_____

Time To Go!

When Mr. Ratburn's class goes to Washington, DC,
  they have a very busy schedule.
Write the time shown on each clock.
Then write a numeral in each star to show the
  correct order.

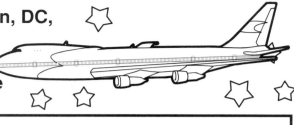

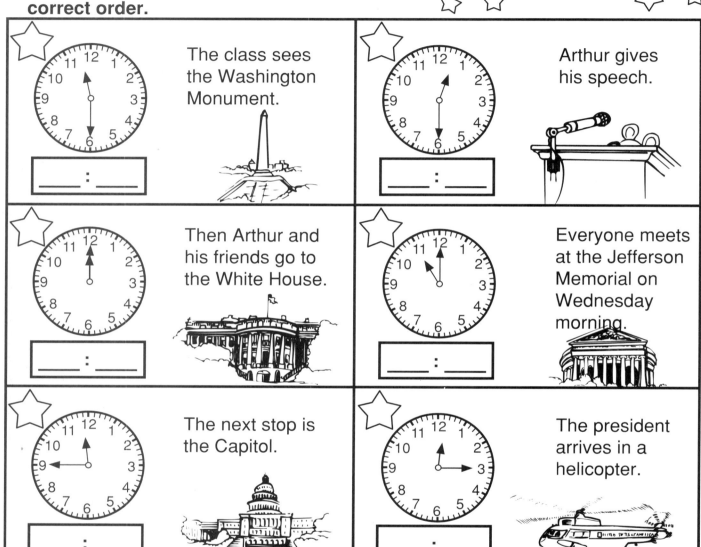

The class sees the Washington Monument.

Arthur gives his speech.

Then Arthur and his friends go to the White House.

Everyone meets at the Jefferson Memorial on Wednesday morning.

The next stop is the Capitol.

The president arrives in a helicopter.

Read each question.
Write the answer on the line.

A. After the class saw the Washington Monument, how many minutes later did they
   visit the Capitol? _____

B. Arthur arrived at the White House at 12:00. How many minutes later did he give
   his speech? _____

Note To The Teacher: Introduce this activity by reading aloud *Arthur Meets The President* by Marc Brown (Little, Brown And Company; 1998).

Thanksgiving

Teach students about Pilgrim times with this cornucopia of skill-based activities!

Pilgrim Prose

Boost creative-writing skills with this hornbook project! Tell students that paper was expensive during Pilgrim times, so children did their schoolwork on *hornbooks*. A hornbook was a board on which a sheet of paper was pasted. The paper was protected because the whole board was covered with a very thin piece of clear horn. Have each student make his own hornbook for a special Thanksgiving writing project.

To begin, give each youngster two 8 1/2" x 11" sheets of white paper. Instruct him to fold each sheet in half twice, then crease it on the folds. Next have him open the paper and cut along the fold lines. Ask each student to cut out a brown construction-paper copy of the pattern on page 18, then stack and staple his papers to it as shown. Share with students a book about Pilgrims, such as *The Pilgrims' First Thanksgiving* by Ann McGovern (Scholastic Inc., 1993), and discuss with youngsters how their lives differ from those of Pilgrims. Next give each student a Pilgrim-related story starter like the ones shown, and instruct him to complete and illustrate the story in his hornbook. If desired, have students use a different story starter on each day of your Pilgrim study. After the hornbooks are completed, pair youngsters and have each of them share his work with a classmate.

- We've been sailing on the *Mayflower* for one month now. I really miss…
- I'll never forget the day we arrived on shore. The first thing I saw was…
- Squanto visited today. He taught…
- I worked really hard today! I…

I worked really hard today! I helped Jacob scare the crows away from the corn. Then I dug the clams out of the mud. That was messy work! The clams were delicious though.

Ben's Hornbook

Feast Your Eyes On This!

Students will cash in on this real-life learning center as they plan a Thanksgiving feast! To prepare, collect several supermarket ads and make a desired number of copies of the shopping list pattern on page 19. Cut out each list and glue it onto a brown paper lunch bag; then laminate the prepared lists. Place the ads, shopping lists, wipe-off markers, and a calculator in a basket at a center. To use the center, a student writes a dollar amount on the budget line of her shopping list. (Provide a budget for each student or have her determine her own.) Then she reads the ads to find desired items and records them on her list along with their prices. The youngster uses a calculator to determine if she has stayed within her budget. She makes adjustments to her list as needed, then writes her total. Have her describe on a separate sheet of paper how she made her "shopping" decisions; then ask her to wipe off her list to prepare it for the next Thanksgiving shopper.

The Pilgrim Promise

The Pilgrims knew that to be safe in the New World, they needed to cooperate and stick together. To help them do so, they created an agreement called the *Mayflower Compact,* the first set of laws in America that said the majority should rule. Forty-one men agreed to and signed the Compact. Have your youngsters follow in their footsteps with this class activity. First brainstorm with students classroom rules that would help them work together in a positive manner. List these ideas on the chalkboard. With students' help, narrow the list to three or four rules. Copy them onto a large sheet of chart paper and have each student sign his name at the bottom. Carefully tear the edges of the paper to achieve an aged look. Then display your class compact as a reminder of your youngsters' promise. For added reinforcement of positive behaviors, present copies of the award on page 19 to students as desired.

Pattern

Use with "Pilgrim Prose" on page 17.

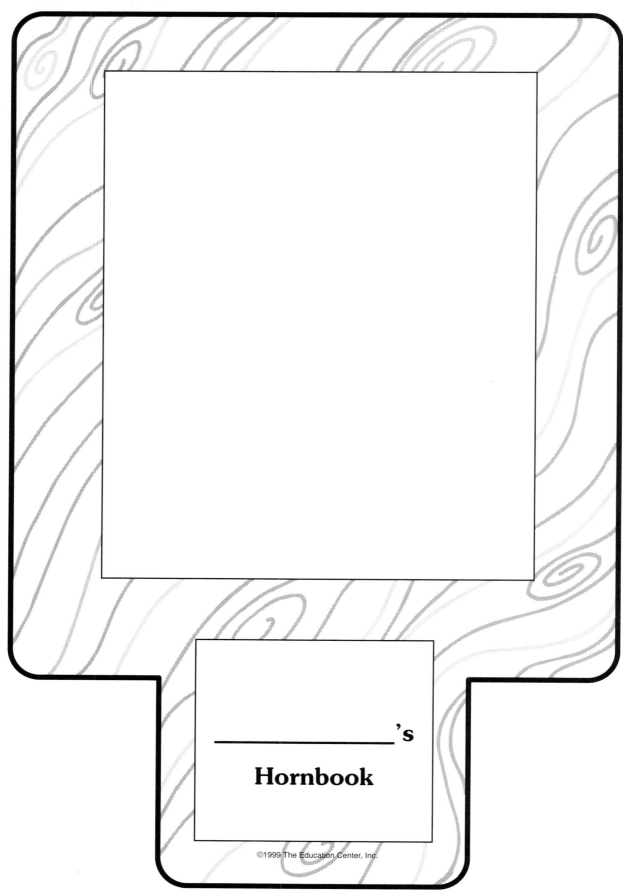

_____'s

Hornbook

©1999 The Education Center, Inc.

Thanksgiving Shopping List

Budget _____

Item	Cost

How much did you spend in all? _____

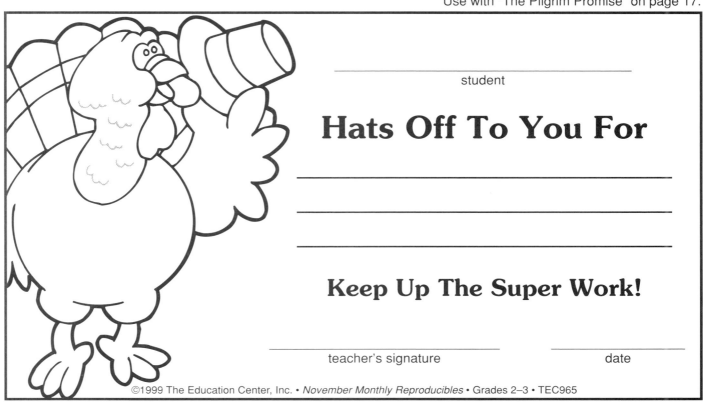

_____
student

Hats Off To You For

_____

_____

_____

Keep Up The Super Work!

_____   _____
teacher's signature   date

Name_____

Horns Of Plenty

**Cut out each picture.
Glue it onto the cornucopia with the matching beginning blend.**

sl _____
_____
_____

sl	sl
sl	sl

sn	sn
sn	sn

sn _____
_____
_____

On each cornucopia, write the names of its pictures.

st _____
_____
_____

st	st
st	st

Bonus Box: Choose five words from above. On the back of this sheet use each word in a different silly Thanksgiving sentence.

©1999 The Education Center, Inc. • *November Monthly Reproducibles* • Grades 2–3 • TEC965 • Key p. 63

Name_____

What A Pal!

This is my friend.
To find out who he is, solve
each problem below.
Show your work.

H	M	O	S
346 + 139	245 + 384	622 + 249	477 + 217
U 327 + 463	**A** 456 + 135	**E** 321 + 649	**N** 817 + 148
S 745 + 238	**Q** 467 + 406	**A** 137 + 523	**I** 593 + 316
I 790 + 191	**N** 378 + 214	**T** 277 + 131	

What is my friend's name?
To answer the question, write each letter above the
matching sum below.

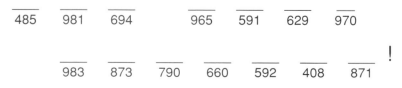

___	___	___		___	___	___	___		___	___
485	981	694		965	591	629	970		909	694

| ___ | ___ | ___ | ___ | ___ | ___ | ___ | !
|-----|-----|-----|-----|-----|-----|-----|
| 983 | 873 | 790 | 660 | 592 | 408 | 871 |

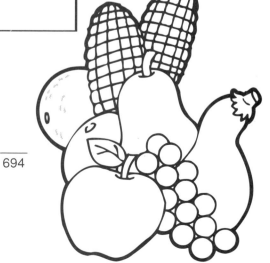

Bonus Box: Find out three facts about the Pilgrim's
friend. Write them on the back of this sheet.

Turkey Day Tales

Read what each person did on Thanksgiving.
Then answer each question below.

Jeff did a great job of saying his lines in the play! He played one of the people who came to America on the *Mayflower*.

Sandy watched as the giant balloons went down the street. Floats with clowns and dancers passed by next. Many marching bands followed.

Becky watched the big game by herself. She hoped her favorite team would soon score their third touchdown.

Joel helped his mom make the dessert. Joel scooped out the pumpkin and he rolled the crust. When it was done baking, he put whipped cream on each slice!

1. What type of part did Jeff have in the play? _____

2. Where was Sandy on Thanksgiving Day? _____

3. What kind of game did Becky watch? _____

4. What did Joel's family have for dessert? _____

5. Who is most likely to be outdoors? _____

6. How many touchdowns has Becky's favorite team already scored? _____

7. What did Sandy see at the parade? _____

8. Do you think Jeff rehearsed for the play? Why or why not? _____

IT'S TURKEY TIME!

What would November be without a few turkeys strutting here and there?
Serve up these fabulous fowl activities that have all the trimmings for success!

The Truth About Turkeys

Teach students a flock of turkey facts with this descriptive writing idea! Read to students a nonfiction book about turkeys such as *All About Turkeys* by Jim Arnosky (Scholastic Inc., 1998) or share the information shown. If desired, have students research additional information about these special birds. Give each student a copy of page 24. Have him imagine that he has been hired to design an informational sign for a zoo's turkey exhibit. Instruct each youngster to use the facts he has learned to write a description about turkeys on his sheet. Ask him to color the illustration as desired. Then give each youngster an opportunity to share his work with a classmate.

Fowl Facts
- Male turkeys are called *toms,* and female turkeys are called *hens.*
- Baby turkeys are called *poults.*
- Turkeys eat seeds, nuts, grains, berries, greens, and insects.
- A turkey has excellent eyesight. It can see a movement a hundred yards away!
- Wild turkeys can fly up to 50 miles an hour. Domestic turkeys cannot fly.
- Wild turkeys rest in trees at night.
- A turkey's head and throat change color when it is excited.

Tasty Turkey Treats

These savory snacks are a snap to make! Have each student prepare her own turkey cookie using the directions shown. As she samples her treat, read aloud a turkey-related story (see "Fine-Feathered Tales" for suggested titles). Gobble, gobble!

Fine-Feathered Tales

Here's a sensational story map idea featuring November's most popular bird, the turkey! Read with students a story about turkeys, such as *Gracias, The Thanksgiving Turkey* by Joy Cowley (Scholastic Inc., 1998) or *A Turkey For Thanksgiving* by Eve Bunting (Clarion Books, 1995). Discuss with youngsters its story elements. Next give each student a copy of page 25. Instruct her to write information on each feather as indicated. Have her color the turkey's head, wings, and feet, and then outline each of its feathers with crayons. Ask each youngster to cut out her completed story map and glue it onto a sheet of brightly colored construction paper. Then display students' projects on a bulletin board titled "Fine-Feathered Tales."

Easy Turkey Cookies

Ingredients For One Cookie:
1 round sugar cookie, approximately 3 1/2" in diameter
approximately 2 spoonfuls of white frosting
a small portion of yellow cake-decorating frosting in a tube
6 pieces of candy corn
3 M&M's Minis® candies
3 red hots
1 thin pretzel stick

1. Use a plastic knife to spread white frosting onto the cookie.
2. Place the candy corn in the frosting near the top of the cookie for feathers.
3. Squeeze a small amount of yellow frosting onto the center of the cookie for a head.
4. Place the M&M's Minis® candies in the yellow frosting for the eyes and beak as shown.
5. Add the red hots below the beak for the turkey's wattle.
6. Break the pretzel stick in half. Near the bottom of the cookie, place one end of each half in the frosting for legs.

The Truth About Turkeys

Write a description of turkeys.
Use at least four facts.

The Turkey

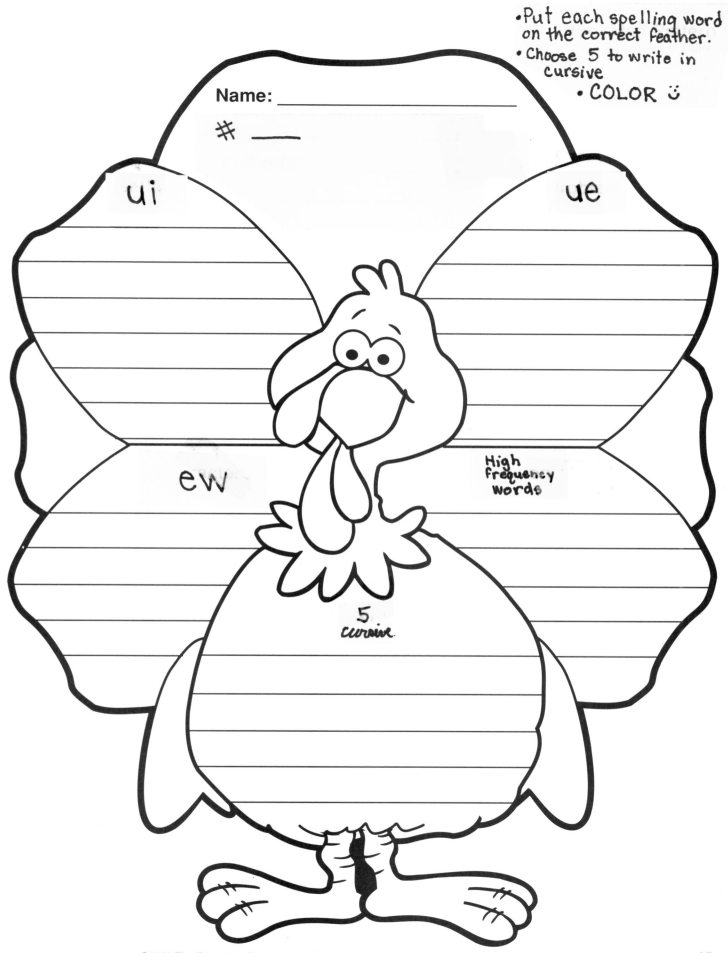

- Put each spelling word on the correct feather.
- Choose 5 to write in cursive
- COLOR ☺

Name: _____

___

ui

ue

ew

High frequency words

5 cursive

Name _____

26

Fine-Feathered Funds

Count the money on each feather.
Write the total on the line.

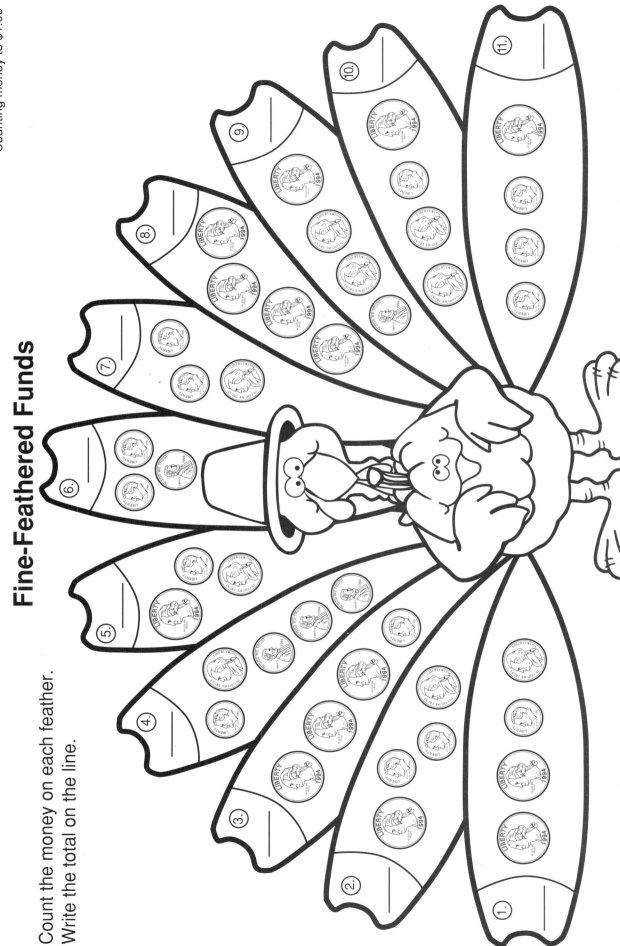

Bonus Box: If the total is even, color its feather orange. If it is odd, color its feather yellow. Color the rest of the picture any colors you choose.

©1999 The Education Center, Inc. • *November Monthly Reproducibles* • Grades 2–3 • TEC965 • Key p. 63

Let's Talk Turkey!

Synonyms are words with nearly the same meanings. For each word, find a synonym in the Word Bank.
Write the synonym on the line.
Then color the picture.

noisy
fast

lovely
fly

fat
hard

Word Bank

bird
nap

delicious
powerful

I'm getting tired. Holding up feathers is hard work!

1. loud _____

2. tasty _____

3. beautiful _____

4. quick _____

5. soar _____

6. plump _____

7. fowl _____

8. sleep _____

9. strong _____

10. difficult _____

Bonus Box: Choose five words from the Word Bank. On the back of this sheet, use each one in a different sentence about turkeys.

27

Name _____

Turkey Tracks

Read the sentences.
Write the correct punctuation in each box.
For each punctuation mark, color a matching feather.

1. Turkeys eat seeds, berries, and insects ☐

2. Did you know that male turkeys are called *toms* ☐

3. Female turkeys are called *hens* ☐

4. Young turkeys are called *poults* ☐

5. Are *hens* larger than *toms* ☐

6. Turkey eggs are tan speckled with brown ☐

7. It takes about four weeks for a turkey egg to hatch ☐

8. How big is a turkey egg ☐

9. Turkey eggs are twice as big as chicken eggs ☐

10. Did you know that only wild turkeys can fly ☐

11. Wild turkeys rest in trees at night ☐

12. Would you like to have a pet turkey ☐

Bonus Box: On the back of this sheet, write a story about a turkey that got lost in the city. Remember to use correct ending punctuation.

NATIVE AMERICANS

Explore with students the fascinating heritage of Native American cultures with these unique projects and reproducible activities.

Native American Gifts

Native Americans were our country's first Americans. When other people came to America, Native Americans shared many things with them. Teach youngsters about some of these gifts with this lunch-bag booklet idea. First, have each student make a booklet as described in the directions on this page. Then give each youngster a copy of page 30. Have him use the Word Bank to complete his sentences. Then ask each student to personalize his cover and color his picture cards and cover as desired. Next instruct him to cut his sentence strips, booklet cover, and picture cards on the bold lines. (He may discard the Word Bank.) Ask each student to glue his cover cutout onto the front of his lunch-bag booklet. Then have him glue each picture card with its matching sentence strip onto a separate page. Encourage youngsters to share their completed booklets with family members.

Fabulous Face Masks

Native Americans had many different beliefs and customs about curing illness. Some Iroquois people wore face masks while dancing and chanting. The masks represented forest creatures with the power to drive away sickness. Share this information with students; then have each youngster make her own face mask. To begin, ask each student to color and cut out a copy of the mask on page 31. Next instruct her to glue the mask onto a piece of tagboard. After the glue has dried, have her cut off the excess tagboard. Help each student cut out the eyeholes on her mask. Then have each youngster glue lengths of yarn or strips of colorful construction paper to the top of her mask for hair. To complete her project, instruct each student to punch a hole at the dot on each side of her mask, then tie a ten-inch length of yarn at each hole. Invite youngsters to try on their masks, before showcasing these creative projects on a bulletin board titled "Fabulous Face Masks."

Lunch-Bag Booklet

Materials For One Booklet:
2 large, brown paper lunch bags (approximately 6" x 12" unopened)
ruler
hole puncher
yarn
scissors

Directions:
1. Draw a line below the flap on each bag. Draw another line approximately six inches below the first (Figure 1).
2. Carefully cut along both lines.
3. Cut off the fold on each bag's right side. Discard the paper scraps.
4. Pull out each bag's fold on the left edge and crease the new fold (Figure 2).
5. Place the bags atop one another. Fold the left edge of the stack over approximately one inch.
6. Crease the fold. Punch two sets of holes through the thicknesses (Figure 3).
7. Thread a length of yarn through each set of holes and tie together.

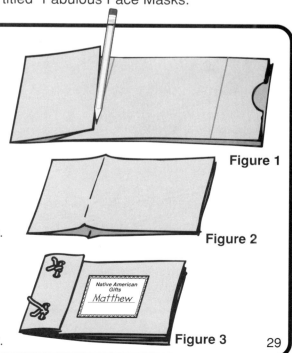

Figure 1

Figure 2

Native American Gifts
Matthew

Figure 3

Booklet Patterns And Word Bank

Use with "Native American Gifts" on page 29.

Native Americans introduced **maize** to the Pilgrims. Today we call this food _____.	These special shoes are called **snowshoes.** Walking on very deep _____ is much easier with them.
Native Americans invented the **canoe.** This special boat is made by hollowing out a _____ .	Native Americans wove many different kinds of **baskets.** Some baskets were used to _____ water or seeds.
Moccasins are shoes that are made with very soft _____. Some moccasins are decorated with beads and dyed porcupine quills.	Native Americans made **pottery** containers with _____ from the earth. Some containers were used for special ceremonies.

Native American Gifts

_____
Name

©1999 The Education Center, Inc.

Word Bank

tree	snow	carry
clay	corn	leather

30

©1999 The Education Center, Inc. • *November Monthly Reproducibles* • Grades 2–3 • TEC965

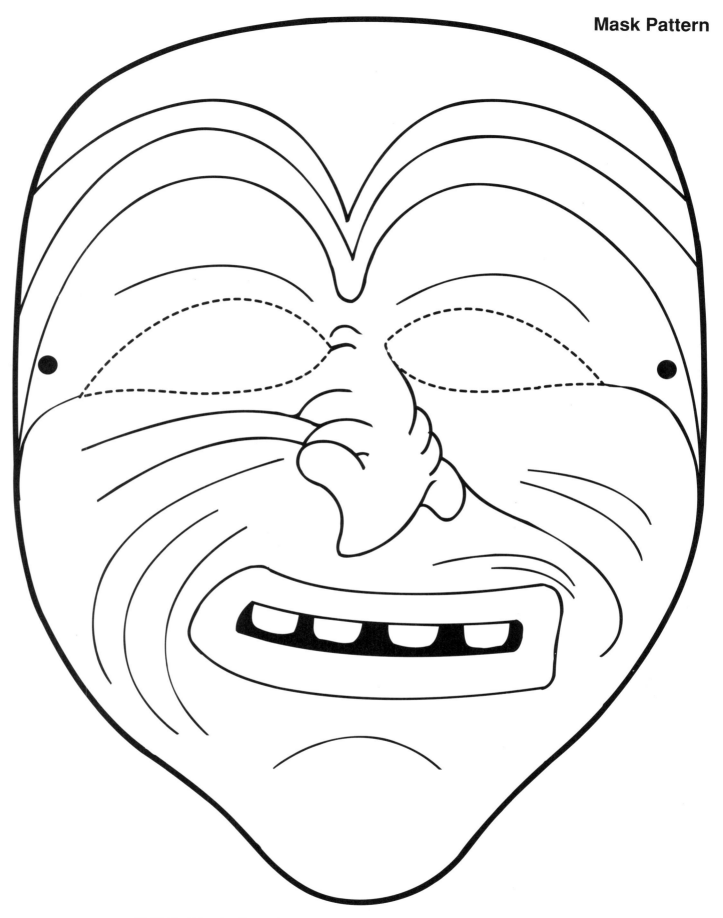

©1999 The Education Center, Inc. • *November Monthly Reproducibles* • Grades 2–3 • TEC965

Note To The Teacher: Use with "Fabulous Face Masks" on page 29.

31

Marvelous Maize

Maize is another word for corn.
Solve each problem.
Use the code to color each answer on the maize.

1. 360
− 210

2. 526
− 214

3. 739
− 122

4. 400
− 200

5. 313
− 111

6. 491
− 100

7. 967
− 712

8. 551
− 230

9. 975
− 414

10. 572
− 162

11. 249
− 102

12. 775
− 325

13. 476
− 124

14. 909
− 606

15. 700
− 200

16. 335
− 132

17. 999
− 743

18. 489
− 326

19. 587
− 423

20. 973
− 142

Color Code:
odd answer = yellow
even answer = brown

Numbers on the maize: 450, 352, 163, 164, 561, 831, 255, 500, 202, 391, 410, 321, 312, 147, 150, 256, 303, 203, 617, 200

Bonus Box: Little Bluebird and her sister picked 220 ears of maize this year. Last year they picked 363 ears. How many more ears did they pick last year? Solve the problem on the back of this sheet.

The Sioux

Read the paragraphs.

The Sioux are a group of tribes who lived in the plains. They hunted buffalo for food, clothing, shelter, and tools. The Sioux were *nomadic.* They moved from place to place, following the buffalo herds. It was important that the Sioux could move their homes easily because they moved so often. These tribes lived in tentlike homes called *tepees.*

Horses were valued by the Sioux. These tribes traveled on horseback. The horses were used to carry tepees and other belongings.

The Sioux counted the years by the passing of winters. During the year, they painted pictures on animal hides to show important events.

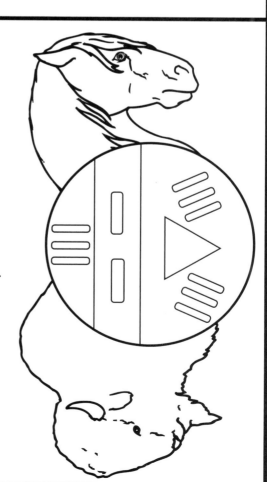

Read each definition.
Find the matching word in the paragraphs.
Write it on the line.

1. moving from place to place _____

2. groups of animals _____

3. tentlike homes _____

4. prized, important _____

Read each question.
Write the answer on the line.

5. Why were buffalo important to the Sioux? _____

6. Why was it important for the Sioux to be able to move their homes easily? _____

7. If you lived with the Sioux, how would you describe your age? _____

    How old would you be? _____

Name _____

Awesome Arrowheads

Solve each word problem on the matching arrowhead.
Write your answer on the blank.

1. Little Running Deer made 10 arrowheads on Monday.
   He made the same number on Tuesday and again on Wednesday.
   How many arrowheads did Little Running Deer make in all? _____

2. Chief Wild Horse made three arrowheads each day for five days.
   How many arrowheads did he make?
   _____

3. Small Wind made 30 arrowheads.
   He lost half of them.
   How many does he have left? _____

4. Flying Bird made arrowheads on five different days.
   Each day he made two.
   Then a friend gave him 10 more.
   How many arrowheads does Flying Bird have now? _____

5. Tender Foot made 50 arrowheads.
   He gave away 10 of them.
   How many arrowheads did Tender Foot keep? _____

6. Big Cloud has 10 arrowheads.
   He made four more.
   Then a friend gave him 11 arrowheads.
   How many does he have now? _____

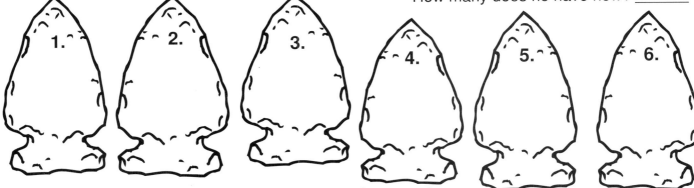

Use a crayon to show your answers on the graph.
Write three sentences about the graph on another sheet of paper.

Number Of Arrowheads									
Little Running Deer									
Chief Wild Horse									
Small Wind									
Flying Bird									
Tender Foot									
Big Cloud									
	0	5	10	15	20	25	30	35	40	45

Colonial Times

Crank up your time machine and blast into the past! Enhance your exploration of colonial America with these fun-filled activities and reproducibles.

Colonial Townspeople

Check out who's who in colonial times! Have each student create a flip booklet of important colonial workers, such as the blacksmith, the tanner, and the hatter. Give each student a copy of page 36. Read with youngsters the description of each worker. Then have each student color and cut out his cover patterns. To make a booklet, instruct each student to fold a 12" x 18" sheet of construction paper in half (to 6" x 18"), then make five equally spaced cuts in the top layer. Next, ask him to glue a cover pattern to the top of each of the six resulting flaps. Under each flap, have each youngster list items that the corresponding worker would make if he were here today. Ask each student to share his work in a small group; then encourage him to show his family this unique colonial times booklet.

jacket
couch
chair
shoes
hat
purse
bookbag

Hear Ye! Hear Ye!

In colonial times, most towns had a town crier. It was the crier's job to walk through the streets calling out the news each day. Use this colonial method of delivering the news to give your youngsters plenty of communication skills practice! On each of several days, select a different student to be the class crier. Supply the crier with important information, such as students' birthdays, lunch menus, or details about special events. Have him summarize this information on a sheet of paper, beginning with the sentences, "Hear ye! Hear ye!" Next, ask the student to ring a bell or beat a drum to focus everyone's attention, then read the news in a loud, clear voice. To extend this activity, have the crier deliver news to other classes at your grade level. Students are sure to request an encore of this colonial act!

Colonial Classics

The Hatmaker's Sign: A Story By Benjamin Franklin retold by Candace Fleming (Orchard Books, 1998)

The Baker's Dozen: A Colonial American Tale retold by Heather Forest (Harcourt Brace Jovanovich, Publishers; 1988)

Colonial Times From A To Z by Bobbie Kalman (Crabtree Publishing Company, 1997)

Samuel Eaton's Day: A Day In The Life Of A Pilgrim Boy by Kate Waters (Scholastic Inc., 1993)

Sarah Morton's Day: A Day In The Life Of A Pilgrim Girl by Kate Waters (Scholastic Inc.,1989)

Cover Patterns

Use with "Colonial Townspeople" on page 35.

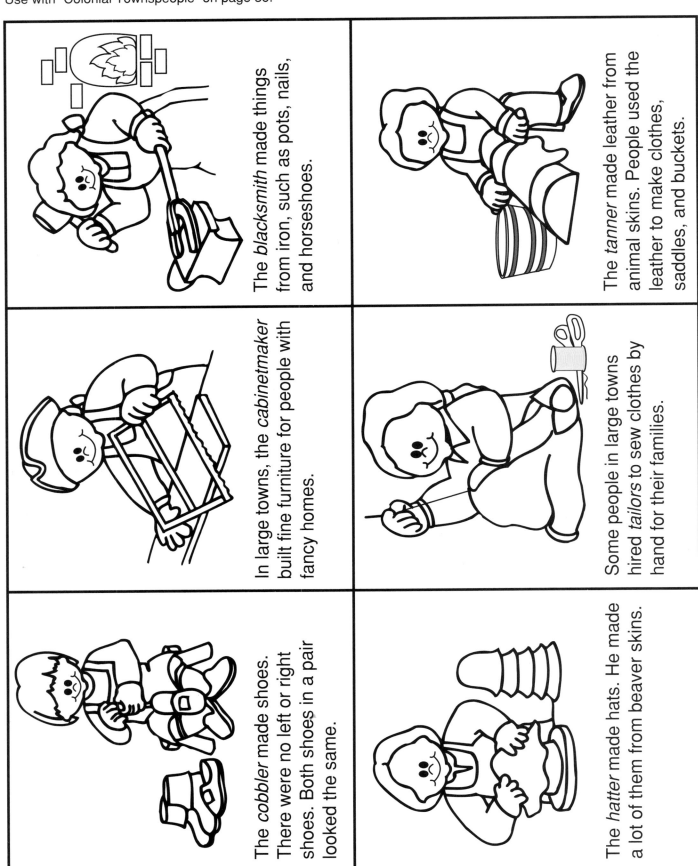

The *blacksmith* made things from iron, such as pots, nails, and horseshoes.

The *tanner* made leather from animal skins. People used the leather to make clothes, saddles, and buckets.

In large towns, the *cabinetmaker* built fine furniture for people with fancy homes.

Some people in large towns hired *tailors* to sew clothes by hand for their families.

The *cobbler* made shoes. There were no left or right shoes. Both shoes in a pair looked the same.

The *hatter* made hats. He made a lot of them from beaver skins.

Name_____

Signs Of Colonial Times

The two words at the top of each scroll are *guide words*.
Write the name of each colonial item on the scroll with the matching guide words.
Write the items on the scroll in ABC order.

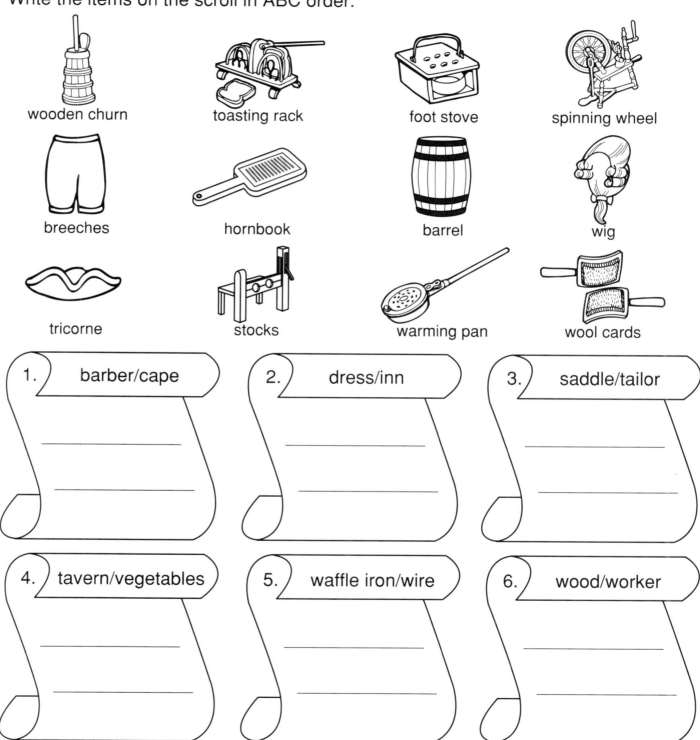

wooden churn

toasting rack

foot stove

spinning wheel

breeches

hornbook

barrel

wig

tricorne

stocks

warming pan

wool cards

1. barber/cape

2. dress/inn

3. saddle/tailor

4. tavern/vegetables

5. waffle iron/wire

6. wood/worker

Bonus Box: Choose the names of five colonial items from above. On the back of this sheet, write a sentence with each word.

Name _____

What's In The News?

Read the town news.
Use your best handwriting to answer each question.

First Wednesday in the month of November

Samuel James will set sail on Friday. He needs two strong helpers to load his chickens and wool on Thursday.

This morning a son was born to the pastor of the church. A daughter was born to Mr. and Mrs. Thomas Hook.

Sir John Latter and his students will present a play to the townspeople today at 1:00 in the town square.

After the play, the keeper of Ye Old Tavern will serve potatoes, turkey, corn, and corn bread from 4:00 to 6:00.

Come to the church on Sunday. There will be a drawing for a quilt at 11:00 A.M.

Everyone is invited to join the events.

1. On what day of the week is the play?
   _____

2. How long will the meal last at Ye Old Tavern?
   _____

3. Who is the teacher in this town?
   _____

4. What will Samuel James take with him on his trip?
   _____

5. How many children were born on this day?
   _____

6. Why won't the students be in the schoolhouse this afternoon?
   _____
   _____

7. In how many days will Samuel start his trip?
   _____

8. What event is planned for the weekend?
   _____

Bonus Box: On the back of this sheet, list five of your favorite class events from this year.

38

©1999 The Education Center, Inc. • *November Monthly Reproducibles* • Grades 2–3 • TEC965 • Key p. 63

PIONEER LIFE

Honor the American pioneers of the mid-1800s with this collection of trailblazin' activities and reproducibles. Westward, ho!

Wonderful Wagons

This wagon glyph activity is sure to rustle up loads of student interest in pioneer life! Explain to youngsters that pioneers traveled across the country riding in covered wagons or walking beside them. A family depended on its wagon and carried many belongings in it. Fragile items were packed inside cornmeal in a wagon *barrel.* Tools were held in the *jockey box,* the seat at the front of the wagon. Sometimes wagons carried about 2,000 pounds! If desired, share with students photographs of covered wagons from *Daily Life In A Covered Wagon* by Paul Erickson (Puffin Books, 1997).

Tell youngsters that each of them will make a wagon *glyph*—a picture that gives information. Give each student a copy of page 40. Read aloud and have each youngster follow the glyph instructions shown. Then ask each student to personalize and cut out her glyph. Display the completed glyphs and a list of the instructions on a bulletin board titled "All Aboard [teacher's name]'s Wagon Train." Each day during your pioneer study, ask a different question for students to answer by studying the glyphs. What a great way to round up listening *and* thinking skills!

Decoupage Pioneer Journals

Pioneer times come to life with this decoupage journal project! Decoupage, the art of decorating items with paper cutouts, was popularized in the mid-1800s. To help each student make a decoupage journal, gather a supply of gift wrap and discarded magazines. Then have each youngster cut small pictures and shapes from these materials. Next give her a sheet of 9" x 12" construction paper and have her draw a one-inch left margin on it. Instruct each student to place the pictures and shapes onto her paper collage-style, keeping the margin blank. Then have her use a paintbrush to cover them with a mixture of equal parts glue and water.

Ask her to write her name on a small piece of construction paper, place it on the decorated paper, and brush the glue mixture over it. Allow the project to dry overnight. Then have each student staple several sheets of writing paper between her decorated cover and a blank sheet of construction paper. On each of several days, share books about pioneers (see "Literature, Ho!" for suggested titles); then have students respond in their journals.

Glyph Instructions

•	**Outline the canvas:**	Use red if you would prefer riding in a bumpy wagon over walking. Use blue if you would prefer walking over riding in a bumpy wagon.
•	**Color the wagon bed:**	Use black if you would prefer seeing a buffalo over seeing a prairie dog. Use brown if you would prefer seeing a prairie dog over seeing a buffalo.
•	**Color the barrel:**	Use orange if you like to eat beans. Use yellow if you do not like to eat beans.
•	**Color the jockey box:**	Use purple if you would prefer sleeping outside over sleeping inside. Use red if you would prefer sleeping inside over sleeping outside.
•	**Color the wheels:**	Use blue if you like to sing. Use green if you do not like to sing.
•	**Color the spokes:**	Use orange if you would prefer playing with beanbags over playing with marbles. Use brown if you would prefer playing with marbles over playing with beanbags.

Literature, Ho!

Wagon Train by Sydelle Kramer (Grosset & Dunlap, 1997)
...If You Traveled West In A Covered Wagon by Ellen Levine (Scholastic Inc., 1992)
Going West by Laura Ingalls Wilder (HarperCollins Children's Books, 1997)
Buffalo Thunder by Patricia Wittmann (Marshall Cavendish, 1997)

Wagon Pattern

Use with "Wonderful Wagons" on page 39.

jockey box

spoke

wheel

barrel

canvas

wagon bed

Pioneer Playthings

Read the paragraph.

Pioneer children played with many different toys. Some, such as beanbags filled with dry beans or sand, are still popular today. Others, such as the whimmy diddle, are not as common now. When a wand is rubbed against this toy, its propeller turns. Another favorite pioneer toy was the jumping jack, a puppet that jumps or dances when its string is pulled. Pioneer children also enjoyed watching the wings or arms on a whirligig spin in the wind. This toy shows the direction the wind is blowing, so adults use it as a weather vane too.

Look in the paragraph.
Follow the directions.

1. Underline the toy that adults use sometimes.
2. Draw a star above the toy that needs a second piece to work.
3. Circle the toy that is a puppet.
4. Draw a box around the toy that is stuffed.

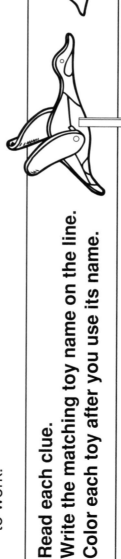
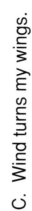

Read each clue.
Write the matching toy name on the line.
Color each toy after you use its name.

A. I come with a wand.
   My propeller spins round and round.
   What am I? _____

B. I have been tossed around since pioneer days!
   I can be filled with dry beans or sand.
   What am I? _____

C. Wind turns my wings.
   I can tell which direction the wind is blowing.
   What am I? _____

D. Long ago I was very popular.
   I can dance and jump.
   What am I? _____

Bonus Box: On the back of this sheet, draw and color your favorite toy. Then write a paragraph about it.

Ginny needs help!
She has lost the prices for the items in her store.
Count the money in each box.
Write the total for each item on its tag.

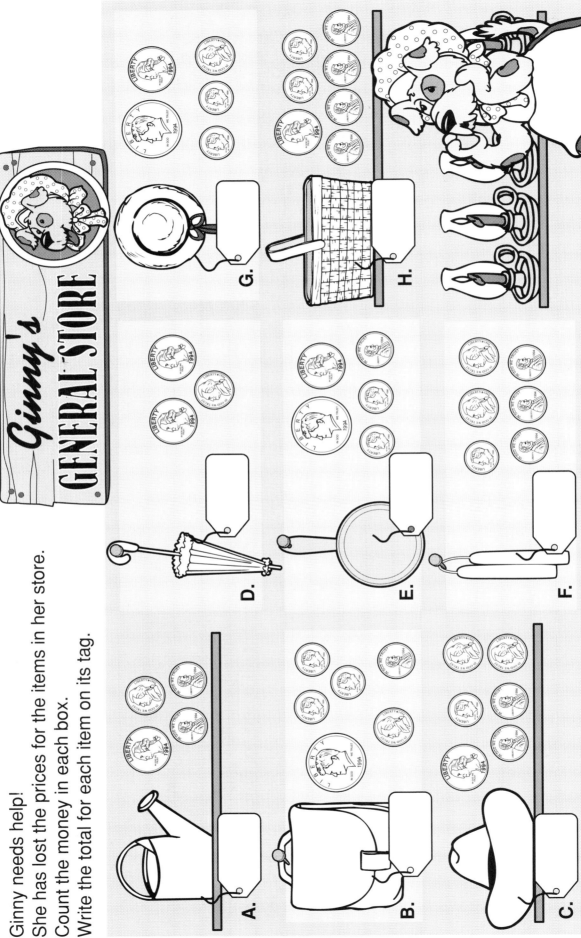

©1999 The Education Center, Inc. • *November Monthly Reproducibles* • Grades 2–3 • TEC965 • Key p. 64

Bonus Box: Find two items that total 78¢. Color them red. Color the rest of the items any other color you choose.

COZY UP TO QUILTS!

Whether they preserve family memories with well-worn fabric scraps or tell about historic events with intricate designs, quilts are cherished keepsakes. Sew up students' interest in this intriguing topic with these creative activities and reproducibles!

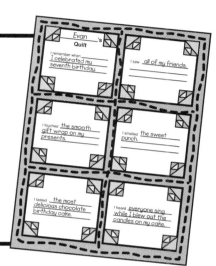

Stories In Stitches

Here's a "sense-ational" quilt idea featuring students' treasured memories! Tell students that a quilt is often passed down from one family member to another as a remembrance of family events. Give each youngster a copy of page 44. Ask him to think about a special memory, then complete the sentence in the first square. In the remaining squares, instruct him to write about his memory, focusing on each of his five senses. Ask each student to personalize and color his quilt squares as desired. Next have him cut out his squares and glue them onto a 9" x 12" sheet of colored construction paper, leaving a narrow construction-paper border around each square. Then ask each student to add stitches between the squares with a black crayon. Give each youngster an opportunity to show his classmates his project; then encourage him to share this special keepsake with his family.

Blue Ribbon Cooperation

Promote cooperation with this classroom quilting bee idea! First read aloud to students *Sam Johnson And The Blue Ribbon Quilt* by Lisa Campbell Ernst (Mulberry Books, 1992). This heartwarming tale tells how an unfortunate mishap causes two rival quilting clubs to patch up their differences and work together toward a common goal. Tell students that like these characters, they will team up with classmates to complete a project. Divide students into small groups. Give each group a large square of colorful bulletin-board paper, glue, scissors, crayons, and an assortment of construction-paper and wallpaper scraps. Ask each group to choose a class or school event from the past. Then have it use the provided materials to make a quilt square commemorating the event. Display the completed squares together on a bulletin board as one large quilt and title it "Blue Ribbon Class Quilt." If desired, celebrate youngsters' successful teamwork with tasty "Quilt-Square Snacks" (see the directions on this page).

Quilt-Square Snacks

You don't need a needle or thread for this delicious quilt idea—just a little creativity and your appetite! Share with students pictures of a variety of quilts and the possible origins of their designs (*Eight Hands Round: A Patchwork Alphabet* by Ann Whitford Paul, Trophy, 1996, is a great resource). Then have each youngster create an edible quilt-square design. To begin, have each student place a slice of bread on a small paper plate. Then instruct her to spread peanut butter or jelly onto the bread. Provide a variety of tempting ingredients, such as raisins, chocolate chips, coconut, and fruit or vegetable slices. Have her use them to complete her quilt pattern. Ask each youngster to name and share her design; then invite her to enjoy her appetizing creation. Yum!

_____'s
Quilt

I remember when _____

_____

_____

I saw _____

_____

_____

I touched _____

_____

_____

I smelled _____

_____

_____

I tasted _____

_____

_____

I heard _____

_____

_____

©1999 The Education Center, Inc. • *November Monthly Reproducibles* • Grades 2–3 • TEC965

44   **Note To The Teacher:** Use with "Stories In Stitches" on page 43.

Name _____

Pattern Sampler

Study each pattern below.
Fill in the blanks to complete it.

1. 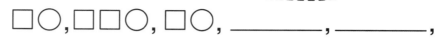 □○, □□○, □○, _____, _____,
_____, _____, _____, _____,

2. 1, 22, 333, _____, _____, 666666,
_____, _____, 999999999

3.

4. 95, 90, _____, _____, _____, 70, _____,
_____, 55, _____, _____, 40, _____, _____

5. ☆ ◑, ☆ ◑, ◑ ☆, ◑ ☆, _____,
_____, _____, ◑ ☆, _____

6. 9, 12, 15, _____, _____, _____, _____,
_____, 33, _____, _____, _____,

7. ○● , ○●● , ○●●● , _____,
_____, _____,

8. 16, 20, 24, _____, _____, _____, _____,
44, _____, _____, 56, _____

Bonus Box: On the back of this sheet, write your own pattern with numerals. Ask a classmate to write the next ten numerals in the pattern.

Patchwork Pieces

Read the **guide words** on each set of quilt squares.
Cut out the **entry words.**
Glue each entry word onto the space with the matching guide words.
Use the color code to outline each quilt square.

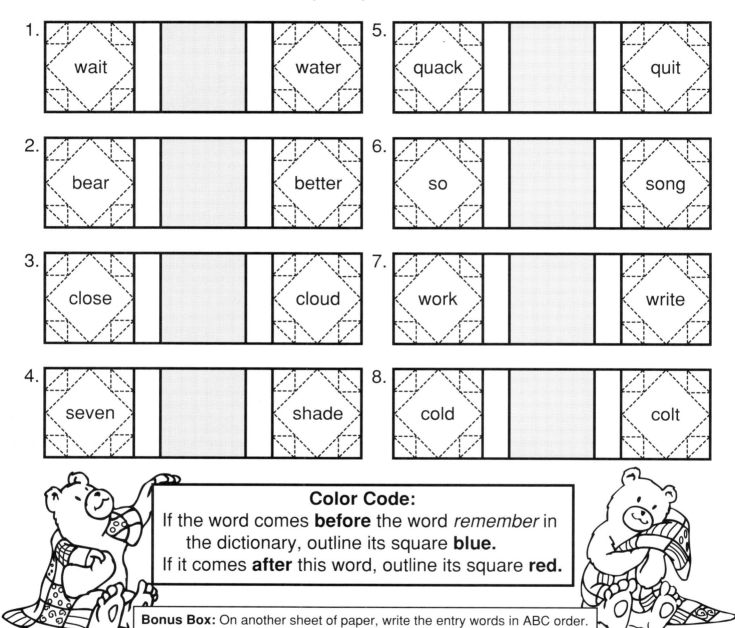

1. wait | | water
2. bear | | better
3. close | | cloud
4. seven | | shade
5. quack | | quit
6. so | | song
7. work | | write
8. cold | | colt

Color Code:
If the word comes **before** the word *remember* in
the dictionary, outline its square **blue.**
If it comes **after** this word, outline its square **red.**

Bonus Box: On another sheet of paper, write the entry words in ABC order.

Entry Words

quilt | warm | wrap | soft | cloth | sew | colors | bees

GETTING THERE WITH GEOGRAPHY

It's a big world out there! Use these ideas to entice your students to explore it during National Geography Awareness Week (the third full week of November).

Picture This!

Youngsters will identify landforms in a snap with this camera booklet! Give each student one copy each of pages 48, 49, and 50. Ask student volunteers to read aloud the questions and answers for each landform on pages 49 and 50. Next instruct each student to cut out his patterns. To complete pages 49 and 50, he glues each answer atop its corresponding question. Being careful to leave the information visible, he colors the booklet pages, flash cover, and camera. Then he stacks the landform pictures, places the lens-cap cover on top, and staples the entire stack to the top of the circle on his camera. Next he stacks the information pages in the same order as the landform pictures and places the flash cover on top. He staples them to the camera as shown. Encourage each youngster to read his booklet aloud to a family member or friend. Now that's learning about landforms in a flash!

On The Move With Maps

This map activity is a surefire "cat-alyst" for geography awareness. Review with students how to use a compass rose and a map key. Then give each student a copy of page 51. Next, for each place on her map, instruct each youngster to draw and color a symbol in a different box at the bottom of her sheet. Then have her complete her map key to match. Ask each student to cut out each symbol on the dotted lines and glue it onto the corresponding square on her map. Then have her follow the directions at the bottom of her sheet. To extend the activity, instruct each youngster to draw a map of the classroom. What a "purr-fect" way to learn about maps *and* cardinal directions!

Exploring The World Through Books

Now that you've piqued your students' interest in geography, share with them these "geo-rific" books!

Where Do I Live? by Neil Chesanow (Barron's Educational Series, Inc.; 1995)

The Mouse Who Owned The Sun by Sally Derby (Four Winds Press, 1993)

Geography From A To Z: A Picture Glossary by Jack Knowlton (HarperCollins Publishers, Inc.; 1997)

Blast Off To Earth!: A Look At Geography by Loreen Leedy (Holiday House. Inc.; 1992)

Booklet Patterns

Use with "Picture This!" on page 47.

Lens-Cap Cover

Landforms

©1999 The Education Center, Inc.

Flash Cover

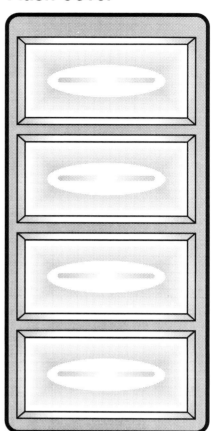

Camera

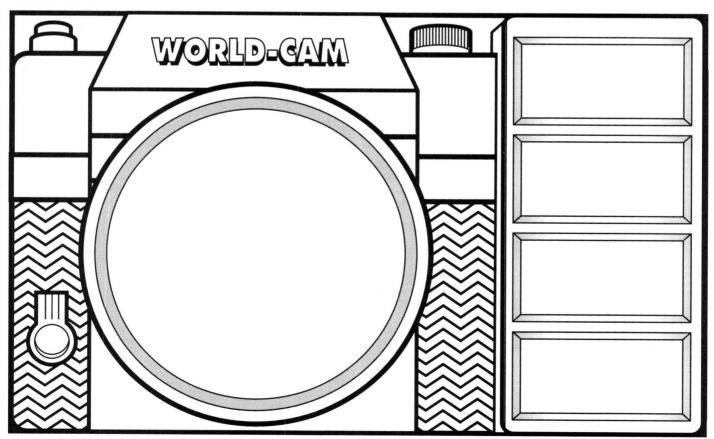

WORLD-CAM

Mountain

Most mountains are wide at the bottom *(base)* and narrow at the top *(peak).*

A mountain is land that rises 1,000 feet or higher above the surrounding area.

The highest mountain is Mount Everest in the Himalaya.

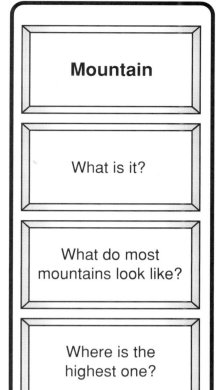

Mountain

What is it?

What do most mountains look like?

Where is the highest one?

Hill

A hill is land that rises above the area around it.

The top of a hill is rounded. It is called a *summit.*

A hill is smaller than a mountain.

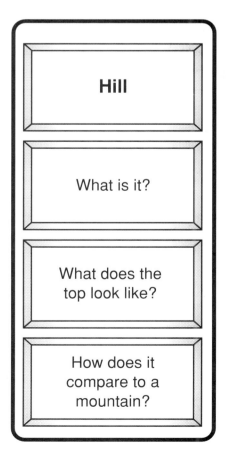

Hill

What is it?

What does the top look like?

How does it compare to a mountain?

Booklet Pages

Use with "Picture This!" on page 47.

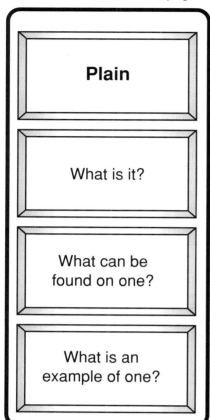

Plain

What is it?

What can be found on one?

What is an example of one?

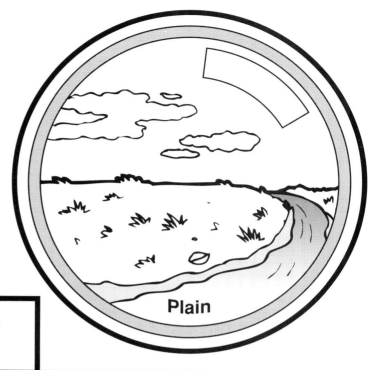

Plain

A plain is a large area of flat land.

A plain is often covered with grass.

A *coastal* plain is lowland along the seacoast.

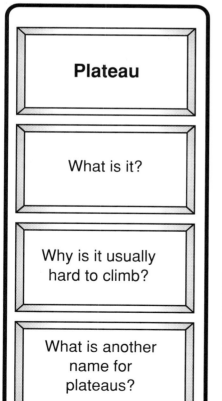

Plateau

What is it?

Why is it usually hard to climb?

What is another name for plateaus?

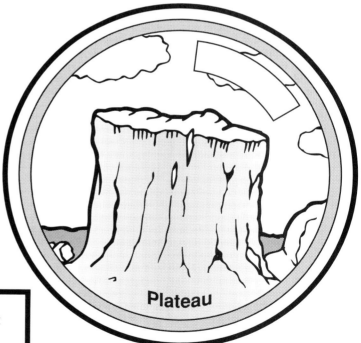

Plateau

A plateau is a large area of flat land that stands above its surroundings.

Plateaus are sometimes called *tablelands* because they are flat on top like tables.

Plateaus usually have steep sides.

On The Move With Maps

**Follow your teacher's directions to
complete the map and map key.**

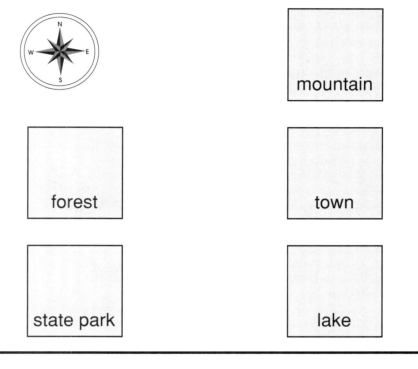

mountain

forest

town

river

state park

lake

Help Cody Cat read the map.
**Write the direction in which he needs to travel to
   reach each place.**

1. From the town to the lake _____

2. From the lake to the state park _____

3. From the forest to the river _____

4. From the state park to the forest _____

5. From the mountain to the lake _____

Key	
mountain	forest
town	river
state park	lake

©1999 The Education Center, Inc. • *November Monthly Reproducibles* • Grades 2–3 • TEC965 • Key p. 64

Note To The Teacher: Use with "On The Move With Maps" on page 47.

Name _____

"Paws-ing" For Directions

Help Katty find the way to her basket.
Complete the directions to show the path.
The first step has been done for you.

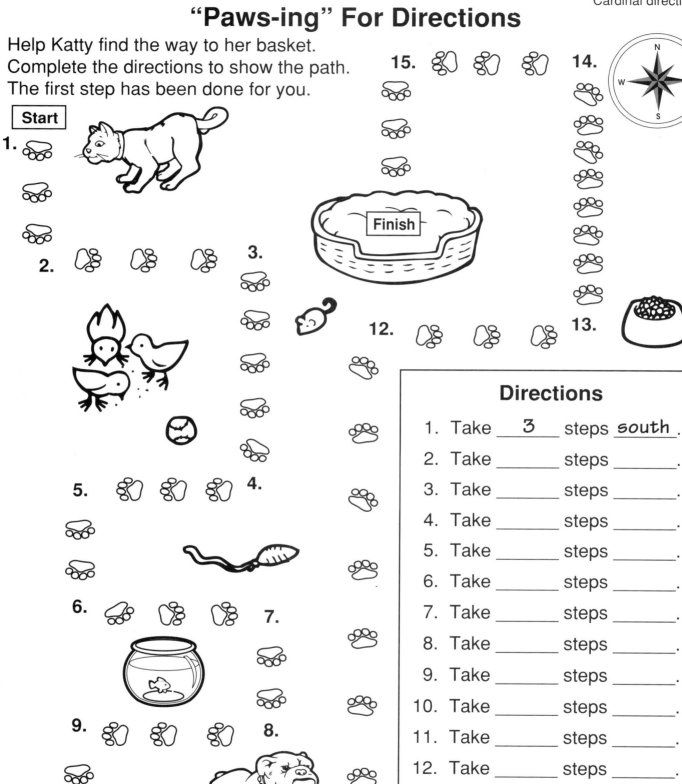

Directions

1. Take ___3___ steps _south_ .
2. Take _____ steps _____ .
3. Take _____ steps _____ .
4. Take _____ steps _____ .
5. Take _____ steps _____ .
6. Take _____ steps _____ .
7. Take _____ steps _____ .
8. Take _____ steps _____ .
9. Take _____ steps _____ .
10. Take _____ steps _____ .
11. Take _____ steps _____ .
12. Take _____ steps _____ .
13. Take _____ steps _____ .
14. Take _____ steps _____ .
15. Take _____ steps _____ .

ANIMALS IN WINTER

Snoozing or on the move, animals' wintertime behavior is fascinating! Explore with students how critters spend the winter with this frosty unit.

A Long Winter's Nap

Your students probably know that groundhogs hibernate, but do they know that bats and lizards take long winter naps, too? Have youngsters investigate hibernating animals with this class book project. In advance, gather books about hibernation, such as the titles listed on this page. Explain to students that *hibernation* is a sleeplike state that some animals experience in winter. A hibernating animal's body temperature lowers and its heartbeat slows down. Since it needs very little energy to stay alive, it can live off body fat.

Divide students into small groups and assign each group a hibernator to research (see the illustration for suggestions). Have each group use the books gathered or other resources to research its animal's winter behavior. Then have it summarize and illustrate the information on story paper. Bind students' completed pages between two construction-paper covers and title the resulting book "Long Winter Naps." No doubt this class book will become a favorite wintertime read-aloud!

Hibernating Animals

bats
chipmunks
dormice
frogs
ground squirrels

hedgehogs
lizards
snakes
toads
turtles

Notable Nonfiction
Hibernation by Paul Bennett (Raintree Steck-Vaughn Publishers, 1994)
What Do Animals Do In Winter? by Melvin and Gilda Berger (Ideals Children's Books, 1995)
Do Not Disturb: The Mysteries Of Animal Hibernation And Sleep by Margery Facklam (Little, Brown And Company; 1989)
Animals In Winter by the National Geographic Society Staff (National Geographic Society, 1998)

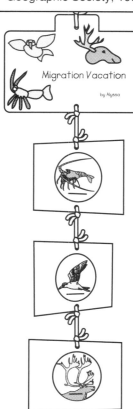

Migration Vacation

by Alyssa

Migration Vacations

Not all animals snooze during the winter—some "pack their bags" and migrate! Teach youngsters about these critters on the go with this nifty mobile idea. Explain to students that *migration* is the movement of animals—on land, in water, or in the air—to places with better living conditions. In winter, many animals travel to warmer climates. Share the migration information shown; then give each student a white construction-paper copy of page 54. Have her cut out the suitcase pattern and complete the sentence on the lined side. Ask her to label the blank side of the suitcase "Migration Vacation," then personalize and illustrate it as desired. Have each youngster punch two holes on the cutout as indicated, then tie a length of yarn to the top hole. Ask her to color and cut out her animal pictures and glue each one onto a different index card. Then have her write about the animal on the back of its card. Help each student use a hole puncher and yarn to attach the cards to the suitcase as shown. Then suspend students' completed mobiles from the ceiling to create a marvelous migration display!

The arctic tern
- is the "migration champion of the world" because it migrates a greater distance than any other bird
- travels to Antarctica in late August
- returns to the Arctic each summer

The spiny lobster
- marches with other lobsters in a single-file line
- travels to deep water to find food in the autumn
- escapes powerful storms by going to deep water

The caribou
- migrates up to 500 miles each year
- migrates south in the winter to evergreen forests
- spends the summer in the Arctic tundra

Mobile Patterns

Use with "Migration Vacations" on page 53.

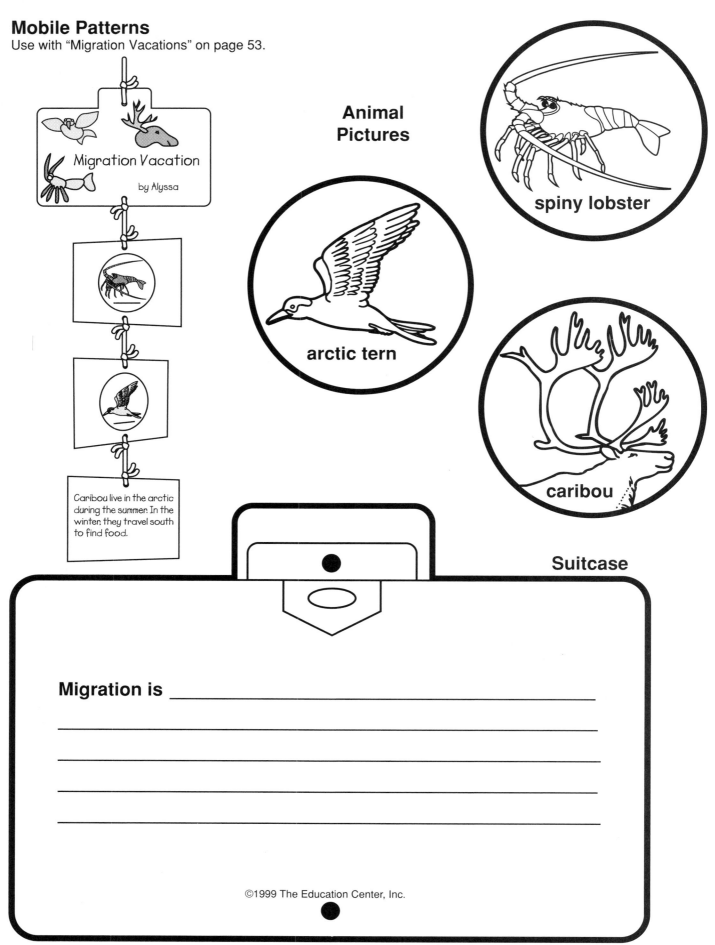

Migration Vacation

by Alyssa

Caribou live in the arctic during the summer. In the winter, they travel south to find food.

Animal Pictures

spiny lobster

arctic tern

caribou

Suitcase

Migration is _____

_____

_____

_____

_____

©1999 The Education Center, Inc.

Name _____

Winter Warm-Up

For each sign, write the words on the lines below in ABC order.
Cross out each word as you use it.

bat	tree	hibernate
caribou	tern	hedgehog
snow	rock	squirrel
den	frog	bear

cave	frost	lobster
mouse	ice	migrate
pond	chipmunk	tracks
snake	turtle	storm

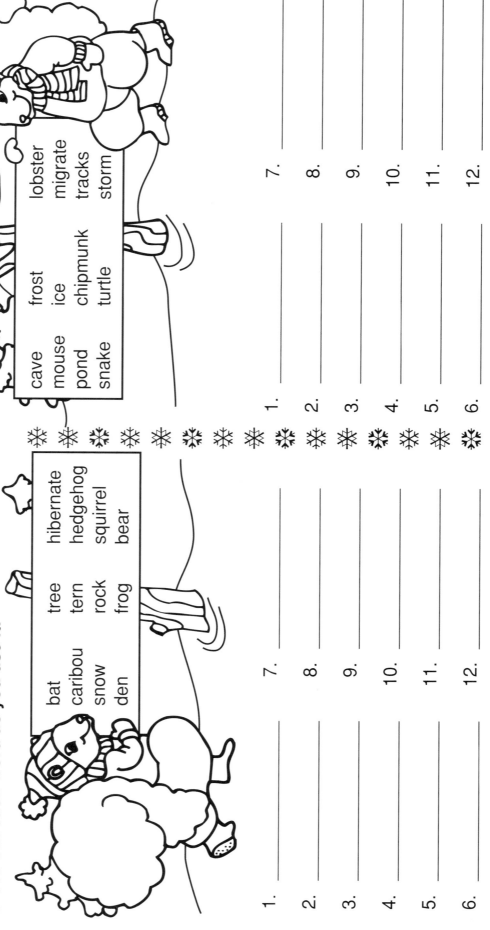

1. _____
2. _____
3. _____
4. _____
5. _____
6. _____
7. _____
8. _____
9. _____
10. _____
11. _____
12. _____

1. _____
2. _____
3. _____
4. _____
5. _____
6. _____
7. _____
8. _____
9. _____
10. _____
11. _____
12. _____

Read the lists.
Find two words that tell what some animals do in the winter.
Use a red crayon to draw a star beside each one.

Bonus Box: Choose one of the animals listed above.
On the back of this sheet, write a winter story about it.

Snowy Day Suffixes

Write the correct suffix *(-er, -ing,* or *-ly)* in each blank.
Color each mitten as you use its suffix.

  1. Snow looks whit_____ in the dark.

2. Snowflakes are fall_____ down!

  3. The raccoon happi_____ catches snowflakes in its mittens.

4. Some snowflakes are larg_____ than others.

  5. The raccoon sad_____ watched the snowman melt.

6. Packed snow is easi_____ to mold.

  7. The bottom of a snowman is wid_____ than the top.

8. The snowflakes slow_____ fell from the sky.

  9. The raccoon is smil_____ because it is wintertime.

10. It has been snow_____ for three days!

11. The raccoon neat_____ packs snow.

12. We have been play_____ in the snow for hours!

  13. The raccoon light_____ walked on the snow.

14. The mittens were neatly hang_____ on the coatrack.

Right side mittens: -er, -ly, -ing, -er, -ing, -ly, -ing

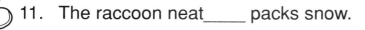

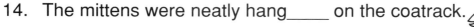

Bonus Box: On the back of this sheet, write five more words that end with the suffix *-ing*.

What better way to capture students' interest than with fun, educational games and puzzles? Try these exciting ideas during National Game and Puzzle Week, the last week in November. Ready, set, play!

Puzzle Piece Picture Frames

Missing pieces to some of your classroom puzzles? If so, put the remaining pieces to good use with this unique frame idea! Cut one cardboard picture frame for each student. Instruct each student to attach puzzle pieces to the front of his frame with craft glue. Allow the glue to dry overnight. Next have each youngster glue a photograph or student-drawn picture to the back of his frame, then tape a loop of ribbon to the frame as shown. Finally, ask him to glue a piece of felt to the back of his project. Now that's a picture-perfect way to use puzzles with missing pieces!

Solve And Toss

Careful subtraction and good aim earn points with this team game! Place a strip of tape on the floor perpendicular to one end of a large chalkboard. Draw and label three lines on the chalkboard and label each line with a different point value. The greatest numeral should be farthest from the tape. Make a class set of subtraction flash cards. Shuffle the cards and place them in a stack. Divide students into two or more teams, and ask one player from each team to keep her team's score. To begin play, draw a subtraction card and ask a player from the first team to solve the problem. If she correctly solves it, she earns one point. Then have her place a large container in front of the chalkboard, below a desired point value. Instruct her to stand behind the tape and try to toss a beanbag into the container. If she is successful, the corresponding number of points is added to her score. Continue play until each student has taken at least one turn. The team with the greatest number of points wins.

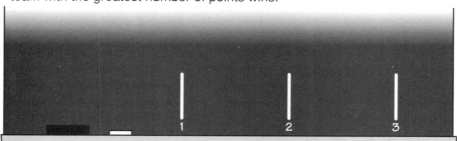

Race For The Cheese

Put a spin on digraph practice with this partner board game! Review with students the digraphs *ch, sh, th,* and *wh.* Then pair students. Give each twosome one copy each of pages 58 and 59, a paper clip, a pencil, and two game pieces such as plastic counters. Have one student in each pair cut out the spinner and word list. To begin play, each student places his game piece on a different starting space. Then he uses a pencil and the paper clip to spin a digraph (see the illustration on page 59). The player moves his game piece one or two spaces, trying to land on a word ending that he can use. Next he tries to name a word combining the digraph and the word ending. If he is able to name a word, he keeps his game piece on the space. (His partner uses the word list to verify the word.) If the player cannot make a word, he returns his game piece to the space where he started his turn. Play continues in a like manner until one player reaches the finish line. For additional digraph practice, have each student take a set of materials home to play the game with family members.

Race For The Cheese

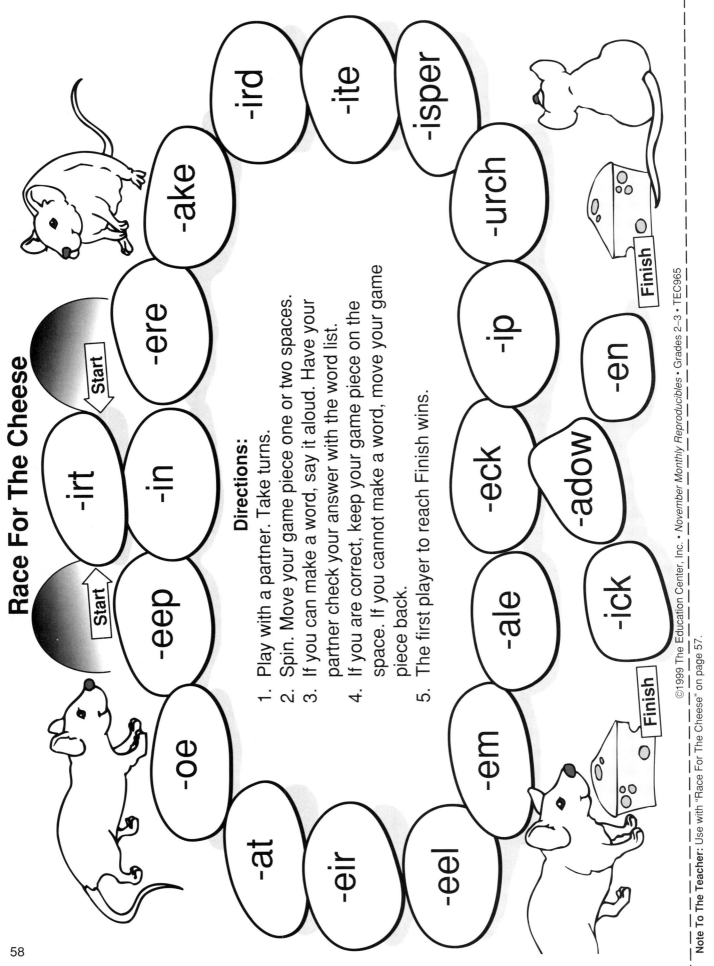

Start

Start

-irt

-in

-eep

-oe

-at

-eir

-eel

-ere

-ake

-ird

-ite

-isper

-urch

-ip

-en

-eck

-adow

-ick

-ale

-em

Directions:
1. Play with a partner. Take turns.
2. Spin. Move your game piece one or two spaces.
3. If you can make a word, say it aloud. Have your partner check your answer with the word list.
4. If you are correct, keep your game piece on the space. If you cannot make a word, move your game piece back.
5. The first player to reach Finish wins.

Finish

Finish

Note To The Teacher: Use with "Race For The Cheese" on page 57.

Spinner Pattern

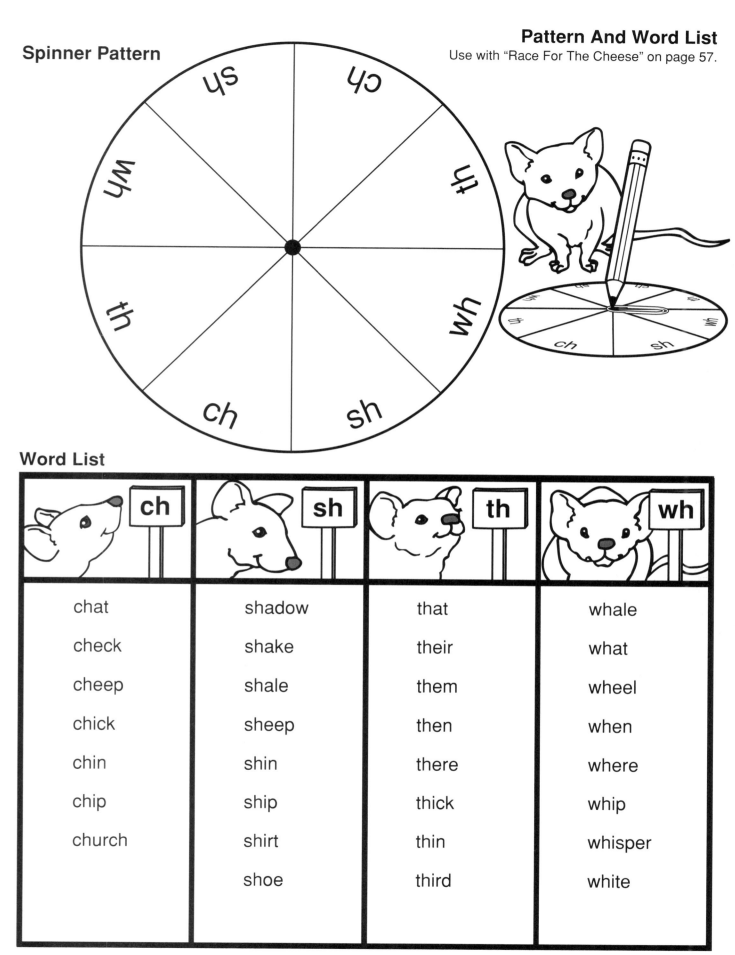

sh ch th wh th ch sh wh

Word List

ch	sh	th	wh
chat	shadow	that	whale
check	shake	their	what
cheep	shale	them	wheel
chick	sheep	then	when
chin	shin	there	where
chip	ship	thick	whip
church	shirt	thin	whisper
	shoe	third	white

Names _____

The Big Cheese

Begin at a space marked "Start." Follow the game rules below.

Circle each numeral as you climb the mountain.

Then, on another sheet of paper, write and solve an equation for the path you took.

The highest answer wins.

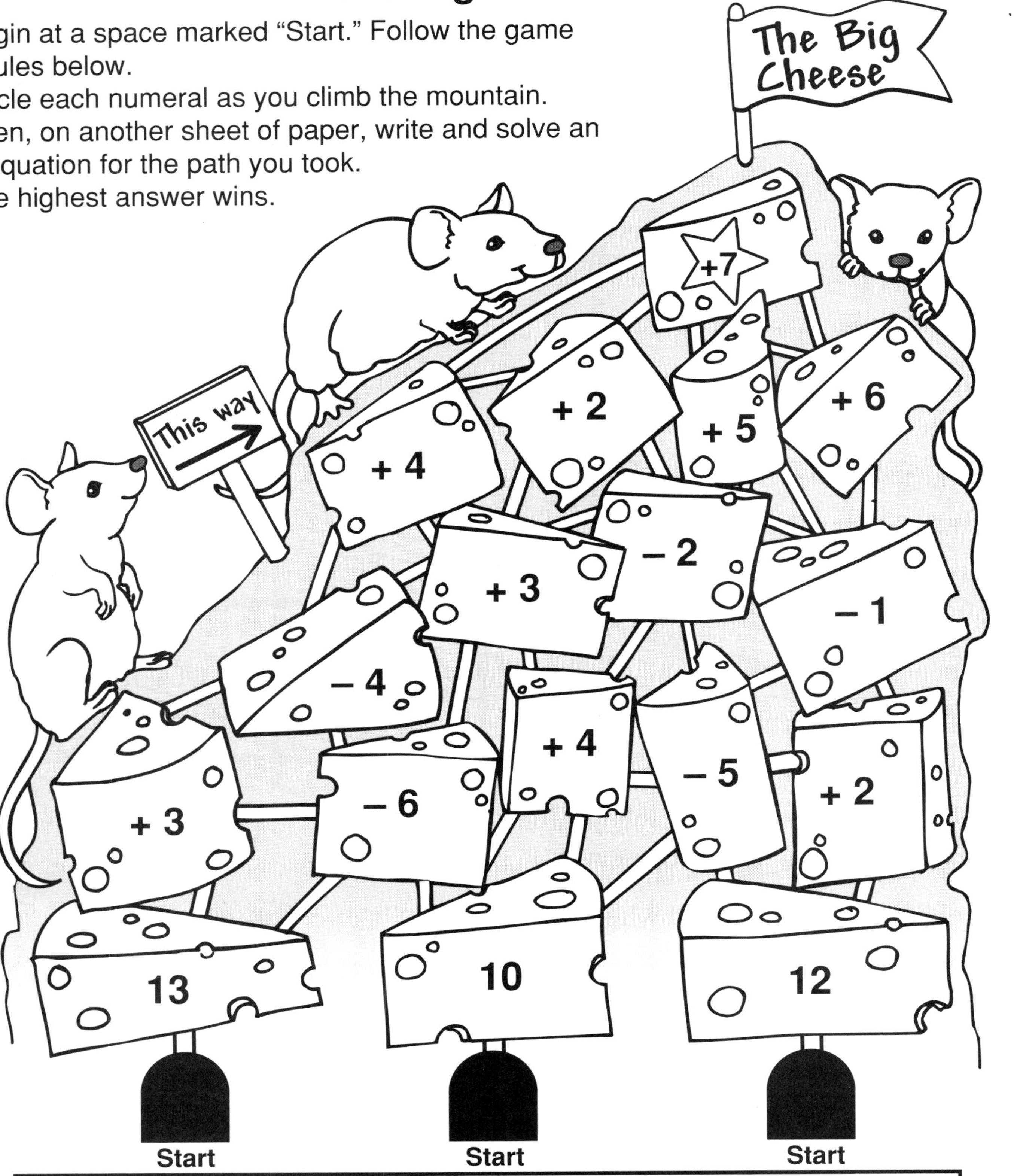

The Big Cheese

+7

+2   +5   +6

+4

−2

+3   −1

−4

+4

+3   −6   −5   +2

13   10   12

Start   Start   Start

Game Rules	1. Follow the lines. 2. Do not move backwards. 3. Each space can be used only once unless it is starred.

©1999 The Education Center, Inc. • *November Monthly Reproducibles* • Grades 2–3 • TEC965

Note To The Teacher: Pair students and give each pair a copy of this gameboard. If desired, have each student use a calculator to solve his equation.

Name _____

Mouse Mix-Up

Cut on the dotted lines.
Read the numerals.
Glue each square onto the grid in number order.

A	B	C	D	E
F	G	H	I	J
K	L	M	N	O
P	Q	R	S	T

Bonus Box: Choose three numerals from the puzzle. On the back of this sheet, write a number sentence for each one.

©1999 The Education Center, Inc. • *November Monthly Reproducibles* • Grades 2–3 • TEC965 • Key p. 64

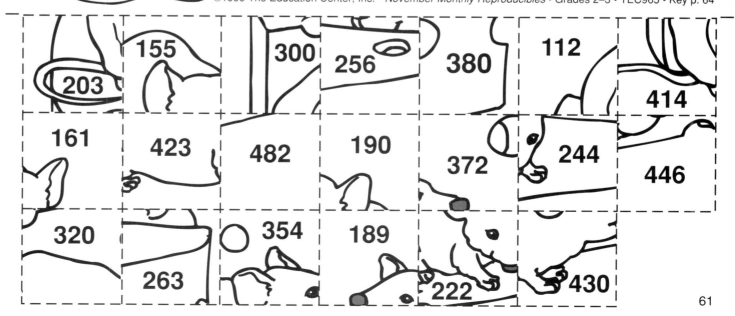

Name _____

Cheese Challenge

Read the words in the Word Bank.
Write each word in the matching block of cheese.

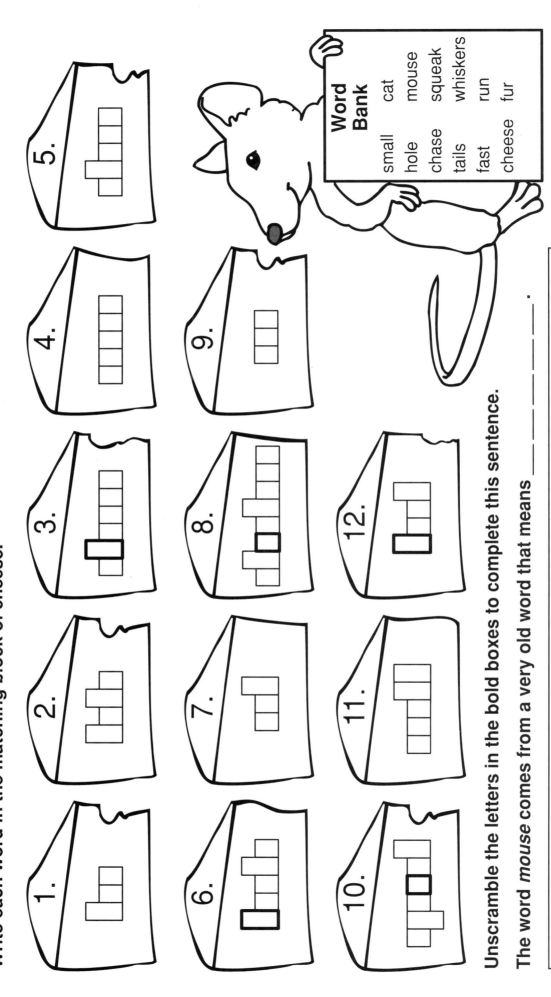

Word Bank

small	cat	mouse	squeak	whiskers
hole	chase	tails	run	
fast	cheese	fur		

Unscramble the letters in the bold boxes to complete this sentence.

The word *mouse* comes from a very old word that means __ __ __ __ __.

Bonus Box: Choose five words from the cheese blocks. On the back of this sheet, use the words in a story about a mouse.

©1999 The Education Center, Inc. • *November Monthly Reproducibles* • Grades 2–3 • TEC965 • Key p. 64

Answer Keys

Page 12
1. $2.50 (red)
2. $.10 (blue)
3. $.16 (blue)
4. $.50 (blue)
5. $3.00 (red)
6. $2.90 (red)

Page 16
The events should be numbered in the following order:
1. 11:00 Everyone meets at the Jefferson Memorial on Wednesday morning.
2. 11:30 The class sees the Washington Monument.
3. 11:45 The next stop is the Capitol.
4. 12:00 Then Arthur and his friends go to the White House.
5. 12:15 The President arrives in a helicopter.
6. 12:30 Arthur gives his speech.

A. 15 minutes
B. 30 minutes

Page 20
(The order of answers on each cornucopia will vary.)
sl: slide, sled, sleeping or sleep, sleeve
sn: sneezing or sneeze, snail, snowman, snake
st: star, steam, stamp, stove

Page 21
H: 485 M: 629 O: 871 S: 694
U: 790 A: 591 E: 970 N: 965
S: 983 Q: 873 A: 660 I: 909
I: 981 N: 592 T: 408
His name is Squanto!

Page 22
1. a Pilgrim
2. at a parade
3. a football game
4. pumpkin pie
5. Sandy
6. two
7. balloons, floats, clowns, dancers, and marching bands
8. Yes, because he did a great job saying his lines. (Accept any reasonable responses.)

Page 26
1. 65¢ (yellow)
2. 50¢ (orange)
3. 85¢ (yellow)
4. 18¢ (orange)
5. 40¢ (orange)
6. 21¢ (yellow)
7. 25¢ (yellow)
8. $1.00 (orange)
9. 36¢ (orange)
10. 45¢ (yellow)
11. 55¢ (yellow)

Page 27
1. noisy
2. delicious
3. lovely
4. fast
5. fly
6. fat
7. bird
8. nap
9. powerful
10. hard

Page 28
1. .
2. ?
3. .
4. .
5. ?
6. .
7. .
8. ?
9. .
10. ?
11. .
12. ?

Page 32
1. 150 (brown)
2. 312 (brown)
3. 617 (yellow)
4. 200 (brown)
5. 202 (brown)
6. 391 (yellow)
7. 255 (yellow)
8. 321 (yellow)
9. 561 (yellow)
10. 410 (brown)
11. 147 (yellow)
12. 450 (brown)
13. 352 (brown)
14. 303 (yellow)
15. 500 (brown)
16. 203 (yellow)
17. 256 (brown)
18. 163 (yellow)
19. 164 (brown)
20. 831 (yellow)

Bonus Box: 143 ears

Page 33
(For questions 5–7, accept any reasonable responses.)
1. nomadic
2. herds
3. tepees
4. valued
5. They used buffalo for food, clothing, shelter, and tools.
6. The Sioux moved frequently.
7. by the passing of winters (Answers for the second part of this answer will vary.)

Page 34
1. 30
2. 15
3. 15
4. 20
5. 40
6. 25

Number Of Arrowheads									
Little Running Deer									
Chief Wild Horse									
Small Wind									
Flying Bird									
Tender Foot									
Big Cloud									
	0	5	10	15	20	25	30	35	40	45

Sentences will vary. Accept all reasonable responses.

Page 37
1. barrel, breeches
2. foot stove, hornbook
3. spinning wheel, stocks
4. toasting rack, tricorne
5. warming pan, wig
6. wooden churn, wool cards

Page 38
1. Wednesday
2. two hours
3. Sir John Latter
4. chickens and wool
5. two
6. They will be presenting a play in the town square.
7. two
8. There will be a drawing for a quilt at the church on Sunday.

Answer Keys

Page 41
1. *Whirligig* should be underlined.
2. *Whimmy diddle* should be starred.
3. *Jumping jack* should be circled.
4. *Beanbags* should be boxed.

A. whimmy diddle
B. beanbag
C. whirligig
D. jumping jack

Page 42
A. 32¢
B. 86¢
C. 47¢
D. 55¢
E. 96¢
F. 23¢
G. $1.00
H. 49¢

Bonus Box: The parasol and beeswax candles should be colored red.

Page 45

Page 46
1. warm (All blocks are red.)
2. bees (All blocks are blue.)
3. cloth (All blocks are blue.)
4. sew (All blocks are red.)
5. quilt (All blocks are blue.)
6. soft (All blocks are red.)
7. wrap (All blocks are red.)
8. colors (All blocks are blue.)

Page 49
(For each landform, the answers should be in the order shown.)
Mountain:
A mountain is land that rises 1,000 feet or higher above the surrounding area.
Most mountains are wide at the bottom *(base)* and narrow at the top *(peak)*.
The highest mountain is Mount Everest in the Himalaya.
Hill:
A hill is land that rises above the area around it.
The top of a hill is rounded. It is called a *summit.*
A hill is smaller than a mountain.

Page 50
(For each landform, the answers should be in the order shown.)
Plain:
A plain is a large area of flat land.
A plain is often covered with grass.
A *coastal* plain is lowland along the seacoast.
Plateau:
A plateau is a large area of flat land that stands above its surroundings.
Plateaus usually have steep sides.
Plateaus are sometimes called *tablelands* because they are flat on top like tables.

Page 51
The symbols will vary.
1. south
2. west
3. east
4. north
5. south

Page 52
1. 3 south
2. 3 east
3. 5 south
4. 3 west
5. 2 south
6. 3 east
7. 2 south
8. 3 west
9. 2 south
10. 4 east
11. 8 north
12. 3 east
13. 8 north
14. 3 west
15. 3 south

Page 55
The first set of words should be listed as follows:
1. bat
2. bear
3. caribou
4. den
5. frog
6. hedgehog
7. hibernate
8. rock
9. snow
10. squirrel
11. tern
12. tree

The second set of words should be listed as follows:
1. cave
2. chipmunk
3. frost
4. ice
5. lobster
6. migrate
7. mouse
8. pond
9. snake
10. storm
11. tracks
12. turtle

These two words should have stars beside them: hibernate, migrate.

Page 56
1. er
2. ing
3. ly
4. er
5. ly
6. er
7. er
8. ly
9. ing
10. ing
11. ly
12. ing
13. ly
14. ing

Page 61
The numerals will be arranged in this order:
112, 155, 161, 189, 190
203, 222, 244, 256, 263
300, 320, 354, 372, 380
414, 423, 430, 446, 482

Page 62
1. fur
2. hole
3. cheese
4. mouse
5. chase
6. tails
7. cat
8. whiskers
9. run
10. squeak
11. small
12. fast

The word *mouse* comes from a very old word that means thief.